BETTER
THAN MESSI?

T0314804

First published 2020 by DB Publishing, an imprint of JMD Media Ltd, Nottingham, United Kingdom.

Copyright © David Clayton

All Rights Reserved. No part of this publication may be reproduced, stored in a retrieval system, or transmitted in any form, or by any means, electronic, mechanical, photocopying, recording or otherwise without the prior permission in writing of the copyright holders, nor be otherwise circulated in any form or binding or cover other than in which it is published and without a similar condition being imposed on the subsequent publisher.

ISBN 9781780916040

Printed in the UK

BETTER THAN MESSI?

THE STORY OF GEORGI KINKLADZE

DAVID CLAYTON

DB PUBLISHING

This book is dedicated to my father, Jack Clayton and my eldest brother, Rowan – for ensuring the family traditions were maintained down at Maine Road

I'd also like to dedicate the book to Georgi Kinkladze, for moments of brilliance I, and many others in Manchester and Derby, will never forget

ACKNOWLEDGEMENTS

My sincere thanks to every City fan that I've chatted to, laughed alongside or argued with about Gio Kinkladze over the past decade. All those views helped in one way or another, even if I didn't agree with some of them. I am also indebted to the following people for giving me their time and thoughts during the writing of this book: Francis Lee, Joe Royle, David Bernstein, Bernard Halford, Shota Averladze, Steve Coppell, Jim Smith, Jon Champion, Neville Southall, Steve Nicholson, Simon Greenburg, Gerald Mortimer, Noel Bayley, Paul Hince, Daniel Izza, Steve Anglesey and many others whom I'm sure will let me know that I didn't name-check them! A big thanks too, to Bill Borrows, author of the excellent 'Hurricane' and former editor of City fanzine 'Blue Print', for writing the foreword for me – I needed another Kinkladze soul mate to get the ball rolling and couldn't think of anyone better than Bill.

I spoke to Georgi several times during the writing of the book but due to his commitments in Cyprus, he never made it home to Manchester during that time. He was a little unsure about the book because he didn't know much about me or my reasons for doing it, but I think he had a much better idea by the time I'd finished. I think he's been let down so many times by people who claimed to have his 'best interests at heart' that his trust is wearing thin. It was a pleasure to finally speak with him and I look forward to meeting him in person one day when I can present his young son Sabba with a junior City kit – well, you have to get them while they are young, don't you?

Thanks to Andy Searle at Parrs Wood Press for agreeing that Gio's biography would make a fascinating story and for extending the deadline on an almost daily basis and I hope I've done my pitch justice! Also, I'd like to express my thanks to Wayne Ankers at the Manchester Evening News for his valuable help in securing the pictures we've included and all the MEN library staff. Simon Thorley has designed another wonderful cover for me and I'd like to thank him for that, too.

There is much of this book I couldn't have done without the help of Dan Brennan and his team at Libero Language Lab, London. Dan, blessed by growing up as an Arsenal fan, was invaluable when it came to Georgi's early days in Tbilisi and with his impressive knowledge of football and contacts in far flung places, from Georgia to Argentina, was invaluable during the research of this book. He uncovered many little known facts about the early life of the young Gio and his family. Thanks also to Robizon Kinkladze, Marina and Kobe Bekeria, Shota Arveladze, Temuri Ketsbaia, Mamuka Kvaratskhelia, Andres Garavaglia, Mamuka Kuparadze, Jim Connor, Irina Abulashvili for all being so frank, open and honest.

To round things off, I always like to reserve my final thanks to my family, because it's they more than anyone else who suffer while I am busy working into the night. For their support and patience, I'm eternally indebted so thanks to my wife/best friend/advisor Sarah and our children Harry, Jaime and Chrissie not forgetting my mum who never gives anything less than total support to anything I do.

HOW AND WHY...

As a kid, Peter Barnes was my hero. I pretended to be Barnsey in the playground and I even had my picture taken copying his smile and pose from a photo Shoot! Magazine. I even asked my Mum if I could have Peter as my middle name and of course, she agreed, albeit as an 'unofficial middle name'. Heroes are wonderful people. Barnes left for West Brom a few years later and I hit my teens soon after. It was over – he didn't play for City anymore, so he no longer held my fascination. I moved on to Eder of Brazil for a while, trying to score banana shots in the same style he did, from acute angles for hours on end with my cousin at the local park.

Long barren years followed watching City with heroes no more than a thing of the past. Approaching 20, I didn't look up to anyone in particular and was stuck in a succession of crap jobs. City's decade matched mine – unimaginative, broke and heading nowhere. Then I got a decent enough job – from a wage point of view anyway, met the wife and settled down. City had a fair team again and going into the mid-1990s, they were almost respectably steady, finishing fifth twice and then ninth in successive years. The Great Unpredictables seemed to be heading for retirement by joining Villa, Spurs and several other top-flight plodders in mid-table land…

Managers had always been a thing of fancy and I paid them little attention, so long as the lads were doing the business on the pitch. Then, in the summer of 1995, reports suggested we were about to sign some from behind the Iron Curtain who had almost single-handedly seen off

Wales – not the hardest task in the world, but still…. He was from a small country called Georgia and he signed on the same day Alan Ball was announced as the new boss – either Bally worked really fast or the chairman had done a deal all by himself. The new lad was to make his debut in the inauspicious surrounds of Raith Rovers' home ground, a few weeks before the start of the new season, though problems obtaining a work permit put paid to that.

Ball reckoned that after watching the player a few times in training, his new charge would have fans hanging from the rafters trying to catch a glimpse. Now Ball's opinion may not have held a great deal of weight with many City fans, but he had managed a player who had captured my imagination and had become a firm favourite of mine – and he played for Southampton - namely Matthew Le Tissier. If Ball reckoned he was as good as Le Tissier, then he'd certainly got my interest. City ran out with Tottenham in August 1995 and I sat in the Kippax, eager to see what the Georgian could do. The team in general was okay, but lacked imagination and I and many others hoped that maybe Kinkladze might be the spark we needed. Being a lifetime Blue, half of me prepared for the new man to be another Kare Ingebrigtsen but the other half was open-minded. Within a few minutes of kick off, a ball was played into Kinkladze and he stuck out a leg and casually flicked it into the path of a teammate with the ease of someone who has supreme confidence in their own ability. Instinctively I applauded the pass and without realising it, I was stood up. I think from that moment on, I went back to being a kid again. We drew 1-1 but I'd seen something out of the ordinary, maybe only briefly, but it was the kind of skill I'd never seen in a City shirt before.

Over the next three years, he never put a foot wrong or misplaced a pass – it was always someone else's fault for not being on his wavelength! Well, that's how it felt for most of us, wasn't it?   As things gradually turned sour for him at City, I wondered exactly what his loyalty to the Blues would cost him career-wise. I saw him do things I've never seen a footballer do and he became the one shining light of a dull side through an awful period in the club's history. Was the club bad for him or was he bad for the club? It's a question that has been asked many times over the years and despite his undoubted genius, his career after leaving Maine Road left me feeling sad. Here was a player fit to grace any team in the world and yet he never fulfilled his potential or followed in the footsteps of his hero Diego Maradona.

As the years have passed, I still reminisce about the days when Kinky performed his magic in a City shirt and have followed his career keenly ever since, hoping that he would find the right manager or team and hit the heights he was supposed to. I was determined to bring his story to the fore again and find out exactly why he never went on to become one of the all-time greats and as I finally became a published author, a book on Kinky was the one I wanted to write more than any other. For situations and events going on around him, I think he's had incredibly bad luck and too many people have gone on about what Georgi Kinkladze couldn't do rather than what he could. This is a player who could excite fans and send them away talking about one particular thing he did almost every time he played – how many footballers can do that? You'll need one hand to count them. So what if he didn't tackle or chase back – you don't need special skills to do that and how often do fans go home saying 'yeah, it was a good goal but didn't No.4 track back well?'.

Football is called the Beautiful Game but there is seldom anything really beautiful in football. Kinkladze created beauty when he played and I really couldn't care about his work-rate or his lack of tackling. There's much more to football than that.

For a generation of City fans, Kinkladze is our Colin Bell. Many of us never saw Colin at his best and in recent years, we've seen Ali Benarbia and Eyal Berkovic play for the Blues – more recently it is Shaun Wright-Phillips. But Kinky was the first player of our generation to really excite and he remains the best player I've ever seen in a City shirt. I needed to talk to as many people as possible to find out more about who he was and what happened to him before and after he played for the Blues. Peter Barnes left for West Brom in 1979 and that was that. Gio left for Ajax in 1998. He's still my hero and for me, the perfect No.10. This is his story.

David Clayton, Manchester, January 2005

CONTENTS

FOREWORD

by Bill Borrows

I MISSED the game against Spurs and then, almost three years later, the final game of the 1997-98 season against Stoke City. In my defence, I was in hospital for the 1-1 draw with Tottenham and, unable to bring myself to witness our almost inevitable relegation to the third level of English football, on a writing assignment in Cuba for the 5-2 win that inevitably arrived just as Manchester City Football Club had left the building.

These games bookend the career of Georgiou Kinkladze. Well, not his entire career. He also spent time at Dinamo Tbilisi, Saarbrucken, Boca Juniors and Ajax. Oh, and Derby County. However, as he explained to the assembled before the last game at Maine Road, 'City is the one club dearest to my heart and wherever I go I'll always love and be grateful to the City fans for the support they gave me.' It was the least we could do. It was, in truth, all we could do.

In a benighted and desperate age bereft of hope, with managers coming and going like gentlemen callers at the backdoor of the Spectator Magazine and expectations lower than a Grandmaster Flash bass-line, Gio Kinkladze was all we had. He was a luxury - like a black-market cut of sirloin in a war-torn city-state or a smoking room in a New York restaurant. Eventually, he became like a piece of floating timber amidst the chaos of a shipwreck. In essence, something to cling to.

Over in Stretford, United were winning pots like they were going out of fashionable prawn sandwiches. 'Eric Cantona is God,' they declared.

It's a toss-up whether their deification of a Gallic cliché with the French equivalent of a Brummie accent was tragic or hilarious. Whichever it was (and both is available at evens with Ladbrokes), there is no doubt that it was embarrassing for the city of Manchester. Their sense of civic pride diluted by the influx of Home Counties and Cockney Reds, all 37 Mancunian United fans fell hook line and sinker for the erroneous belief that France = some unattainable form of arrogant superiority.

In Manchester 14 you could not find one City fan, an all together more knowledgeable electorate, who would swap the mercurial Georgian genius for the pompous, puffed-up French fool. The media would tend to side with Cantona (and trust me when I tell you that it would be difficult to underestimate the number of journalists from outside Manchester who support United – it demeans the profession even further but there's nothing I can do about it at the moment. And no, of course they never go to Old Trafford).

Personally speaking, I'll go with the opinion of Diego Armando Maradona who saw Kinkladze when he was at Boca Juniors and never forgot about him. Had the latter enjoyed his time in Argentina, he would never have made it to Maine Road. Real Madrid, Atletico Madrid and AC Milan also wanted Gio. By comparison, Cantona was asked to take a trial before Sheffield Wednesday could decide to take a chance on him.

This is the difference.

Cantona achieved more in his career but he was surrounded by other great players in a team with forward momentum.

Kinkladze was playing with lesser talents. He would beat three players and look up to find the rest of team-mates watching him with ill-disguised and ill-timed admiration. At times you wanted to chastise them and shout out, 'We pay to watch, you're paid to play' but somehow the words always got caught in the throat. You were also mesmerised. I was there when he tortured a Southend defender who eventually fell over and feigned injury rather than mark Kinky and I was there when we got relegated from the Premiership against Liverpool.

That said, I was not there at the birth and then contrived to miss the final curtain. An apposite bow to the crowd as Gio sank to his knees in tears as his second relegation with the club became a dry piece of historical fact. He played for City for three years, during which time we were relegated twice. I missed Billy Meredith, Peter Doherty and Bobby Johnstone but made it in time to catch Colin Bell, Peter Barnes and Paul Lake. And now Shaun Wright-Phillips.

Georgiou Kinkladze remains the most breathtaking player it has ever been my privilege to pay to watch.

Bill Borrows, London, January 2005

"City is the one club dearest to my heart and wherever I go I'll always love and be grateful to the City fans for their support they gave me."

Georgi Kinkladze, May 2003

"Great players often pay a heavy price for their gift from God."

Diego Maradona, 1996

Chapter 1
PRIDE AND PREJUDICE

"He had a certain innate instinct about when to pass the ball at exactly the right second. He had a natural ability to read the game."

– Robizon Kinkladze

A brief history of Georgia:

Tbilisi or sometimes 'Tiflis' is the capital city of Georgia, located on the Kura (Mtkvari) river. The city has more than 1,300,000 inhabitants and was first founded in the 5th century by the King of Georgia Vakhtang I Gorgasali. Tbilisi has been occupied by many foreign rulers, including Persians, Arabs and Seljuks (Turks). In 1122, after heavy fighting, the troops of the King of Georgia, David the Builder entered Tbilisi. After this battle David moved his residence from Kutaisi to Tbilisi, making it his capital. In 1801, it was ceceded from Persia and came under Russian control. In 1918-1921 Georgia was independent, and Tbilisi functioned as the capital city. In 1921 the Democratic Republic of Georgia was occupied by the Soviet Russia and it would be 70 years before it regained its independence but the Georgian people will never forgive Russia for the occupation. Never.

Its loyal and tolerant people fought bravely as the Red Army soldiers in the Second World War, with 700,000 Georgians battling against the Nazis and more than 200,000 died in battle between 1941 and 1945. During the Perestroika reforms of the late 1980s, of which the Georgian minister of USSR for foreign affairs, Eduard Sheverdnadze was one of the main archeitects, Georgia developed a multi-party system that strongly favoured independence and staged the first multiparty elections in the Soviet Union on October 28, 1990. Shortly before the Soviet Union collapsed, on April 9, 1991 Georgia declared its independence leading to widespread inter-ethnic violence that made Georgia a dangerous place to live and work. Russian supported sepratists became embroiled in what amounted to civil war and today, the country is still not entirely stable, with the massacre by Chezian rebels in Georgia horryfying the country and the rest of the world as more than 400 lost their lives in the horrific siege at a school.

With less than five million inhabitants in total, Georgians are a loyal people, fiercely proud of their battle for independence and refusal to be downtrodden or bullied. Many lost their lives along the way and though organised crime is still rife on the streets of the beautiful capital of Tbilisi, when the national anthem – the Tavisupleba – plays, you are unlikely to find a prouder people anywhere in the world.

Georgians never forget their friends…

Robizon Kinkladze was from a small town in Western Georgia called Ozurgeti, which is less than 50 kilometres from the Black Sea. In 1964, when he was 19, he moved to Tbilisi to study at the Sports Education Institute. Soon after, he then met a local girl, Khatuna Abashidze, who was just 14. In 1968 when she was 18 and had finished school, they got married and not long after, they had a first child – a daughter – whom they named Marina. The Kinkladze family was happy and settled and though they were not wealthy, they felt they had everything they needed. Then on July 6, 1973, their son Georgi was born. Curiously enough, one of the doctors at the hospital where Georgi was born was the father of Alexander Iashvili, who would later go on to play alongside Georgi in the Georgian national side.

In those days, bizarre Soviet rules dictated that the father of a newly born baby wasn't allowed to see their child for the first week. But, three days after Georgi was born, Robizon managed to sneak into the hospital and catch a secret glimpse of his son. "He's got bandy legs - he'll make a good footballer," he thought to himself when he saw Georgi for the first time. Little could he have known how good Georgi would be but his father was determined his son would become one of the most gifted players Georgia would ever produce.

Not long after they returned home, incredibly, Georgi began crawling! They would leave him in one room and within minutes, he had crawled his way into another room - and his leggings were always full of holes at the knees. As soon as he could stand up on his own, Robizon rolled a football to the infant and the 2-year-old Georgi trapped it with his left foot, much to the amazement of his father, since nobody else in the family was left-handed or left-footed. In fact, in those days - because of an idiotic and archaic Soviet decree - it was actually illegal to be left-handed. Everyone was forced to write with his or her right hand. In 1977, Inter Milan came to Tbilisi to play Dinamo in the UEFA Cup at the newly built Boris Paichadze National Stadium. Robizon decided to make the short journey to the ground with his four-year-old son. With a huge crowd of around 100,000 fanatical Dinamo fans making space a premium, Georgi perched on his dad's shoulders so that he could see what was happening on the pitch. Whenever there was an attack on goal, the little boy started kicking with his legs so hard, that his dad felt bruised and sore by the end of the match.

"From that moment on I knew that this was not just a vague interest. He really wanted to play football," recalled Robizon. "And from then on, right up until he was 15 or 16, I worked very hard with him."

The Kinkladzes were an ordinary Georgian family, and Georgi in many ways had an ordinary childhood. Robizon as an engineer worked about 60km from Tbilisi but every day he would hurry back to see his son train at the Young Dinamo football school. Robizon would never let his son see him but instead would hide behind the fence surrounding the pitch. But then, in the evenings back home, he would go over every mistake his son was making - much to Georgi's surprise and puzzlement. 'How could he know what mistakes I am making', he thought to himself, 'when he doesn't even see me play?'

Every day, his father would make up fresh fruit and vegetable juice for his son to drink to build up his fitness and give him enough natural fuel to keep him going throughout the day. He would create a juice made from apple, pear, pomegranate, and beetroot juices. It was not easy. Fresh fruit and vegetables were difficult to come by and were expensive, too. But still, Robizon would always manage to make up one litre of juice every day for his son. And whenever he had time off, he would take his son to various locations to learn his craft further.

"Whenever we had free time, I took him to the resorts, to the sea or up to the mountains to train," Robizon confirmed. "He was never without a ball. We lived on the seventh floor, but I never let him go up in the lift. He had to bring the football up with his feet; he couldn't pick it up in his hands."

All the intense and unconventional coaching practices were about to pay off. On September 5, 1979, Robizon took Georgi to the stadium of Young Dinamo to meet with the coach, Antandbil Kheladze, who was a former player. At the time, again because of Soviet law, it was forbidden to simply turn up and enrol in a football school with bureaucracy ruling or restricting almost every aspect of Georgian life. Everything had to be done according to various regulations and centrally approved – leading to yet further disdain towards the Soviet Union. But Robizon asked his good friend Borya Ichinoa, who had been a Soviet champion in 1964 to help out. He took him to see Antandbil but his first reaction was that he had 50 kids there and that Georgi was too young, anyway. He felt it was pointless to continue but because of his friendship with Borya he shrugged his shoulders and said: "Okay, let's see what he can do."

Georgi was given a ball, and he started to juggle with it. The coach just stood watching, open-mouthed as the six year-old continued to keep the ball up with consummate ease and looked as though he could do it all day long, too. Antandbil said to Robizon that any kid who could control the ball the way Georgi did could walk straight into his academy. Robizon's work was far from finished and he decided to enrol his son in traditional Georgian dance classes (Mtuluri) to further hone his unique ability (perhaps this is why he sometimes plays like he is dancing?). The Mtuluri is a bit like the river dance with very quick feet movements and Georgi was one of the best in the ensemble and many believed he could go on to represent the Georgian national ballet. But both his mother and the dance instructor were opposed to the football and when Robizon was away on work commitments, Khatuna would hide her son's boots! There was only ever going to be one winner, however.

"The idea behind getting him doing the dancing was to improve his footwork and coordination," said Robizon. "He went to classes for three or four years. It really helped him. No other players were doing that - it was my idea. He carried on until he was around 13. He was very talented, and danced solos. They wanted him to stay on and become a dancer, but all he wanted was to become a footballer.

"It was when he was 13 that I knew for the first time for sure that he would become a top player. I helped to give him the speed and the strength, but the football brain was something nobody could teach him. That was inborn. You can't teach that. He had a certain innate instinct about when to pass the ball at exactly the right second. He had a natural ability to read the game."

Marina Kinkladze, Georgi's sister recalled the early days when her younger brother first showed talent with a ball and is in no doubt as to who was behind him becoming the player he eventually did

"I'm his only sister so we have always been very close and, of course, I was with him throughout the time he was in Manchester," said Marina. "Ours was a typical Georgian family – we were very close. Georgi was always a very quiet, modest person. But he was always very popular, always surrounded by lots of friends.

"Dad played a huge part in making Georgi a footballer. He was so dedicated and worked really hard with him. Soon after he started to play football, he started to take dancing lessons to help him with football. It's a traditional Georgian dance, from the mountain regions, called Mtuluri. The movement he learnt doing the dancing is very suited to football and he was very talented at it.

"But then he was always very special when it came to various sports. Despite his height, he was a fantastic volleyball player too. And I remember once at the swimming pool, a coach came up to him and said he could be a top-level swimmer. But he always had his heart set on football."

Near the Kinkladze family flat was School Number 155. That is where Khatuna, Georgi's mother worked as a teacher. Georgi was always a very good student, as he didn't want to upset his mother but at home he had to work hard, too. Robizon forced Georgi, in order to make his knees strong, to walk around the whole flat on his knees. It was very hard for him, but he did as his father said because he trusted his judgement implicitly. His mother was always against that particular type of 'strengthening' and she said to Robizon that he was mad, and it was very bad for their son.

In one room, his dad prepared a mini-gym with parallel rings and ensured he did so many press ups every day. This meant that Georgi was also a very strong-arm wrestler and whenever the kids in the street would wrestle, Georgi was always the best. There were more daily exercises, too. Robizon made him sit first on one leg and then the other to develop his muscles. The natural talent was beginning to blossom and physically, nobody was going to push Georgi around in the street or, more importantly, on the football pitch.

Chapter 2
THE PIED PIPER

"Word had already got out about him by then and half of Tiflis used to turn up to watch him. He was absolutely brilliant; nobody could get the ball off him."

– Shota Averladze

Georgi Kinkladze was born in the Dedube district of Tbilisi, within spitting distance of Dinamo Tbilisi's stadium. Having progressed from the very young junior teams, he was now drawing big crowds wherever he played and was tagged as the most exciting new talent in Tbilisi. His technical skill, dribbling ability and physical strength made him a formidable talent on the pitch and he was already finding his age group little challenge. One of his childhood friends, who would also go on to make a great career for himself, was Shota Averladze who would eventually go on to play for Ajax and later Glasgow Rangers.

"We were both together for a lot of the time as youth players in Tiflis *(traditional name for Tbilisi, still used by many Georgians)*," he said. "I went to School Number 35 which was a famous football school, while Georgi was at the Dinamo Academy. The Dinamo Academy was famous, not just in Georgia, but the whole of the Soviet Union, and it was where every good youth player ended up. Our teams used to play each other – everyone used to come and watch the games and Georgi always stood out as the best player. Then I moved to Dinamo and we played together for their second team when we were aged around 16."

Mamuka Khvaratskhelia was the Press Officer for the Georgian Football Association and a good friend of Robizon Kinkladze. The pair met when they were sent to guard Tbilisi Airport during the civil war, which was bracing itself for a terrorist attack. He recalls how his friend's son first captured his imagination. "Georgi was 16 when I first saw him," said Khvaratskhelia. "He was playing for Mretebi in the very first year of the Georgian national championship back in 1989. It was also my first year as a football journalist. He then went on to play for Dinamo's second team, which was no mean feat as they were very hard to get into."

When Georgi returned home, he was never too far away from a football and his neighbours were the Djordjikashvilis who lived in the same apartment block. Koba Djordjikashvilis saw him playing football in the street with the other local kids, and realised straight away that this was an extremely talented young footballer. So he took him to Mretebi Tbilisi, the smaller of the Tbilisi clubs and therefore the perfect team for him to get a foot on the ladder with. The coach of Mretebi, Vazha Chkaizadze, was a very interesting character. He wasn't just a football coach, but a theatre director, too and in 1988, under his guidance, Mretebi became the first ever professional football club, not just in Georgia but the whole of the Soviet Union which was quite a feat for one of the country's less glamorous teams

"We played in the Second Division of the Soviet league," said Shota Averladze. "Georgi went to Mretebi Tblisi, the first ever official professional club in the former Soviet Union in 1989. In practice, all the clubs were professional in that players were being paid, but this was the first club that was openly professional.

"Georgi had a fantastic couple of years with Mretebi and helped them gain promotion to the Georgian Premier Division. Word had already got out about him by then and half of Tiflis used to turn up to watch him. He was absolutely brilliant; nobody could get the ball off him."

In his first season with Mretebi, Kinkladze played 20 games and scored four goals – he was still just 16 years old. His second season at Mretebi he was even more effective, playing 30 times and scoring five goals. It was then the club he had blossomed at as a young boy, Dinamo, decided it was time he came 'home'.

"By the time Georgi returned to Dinamo, me and my brothers Revaz and Archil were already playing for the first team," said Averladze. "The transfer fee was one million roubles, which was huge money at the time. Mretebi no longer exist – that's because of the financial problems caused by Georgi's transfer – nothing to do with him - but a dispute between the two clubs. Dinamo said that because Kinky had come up through their youth system, they weren't going to pay the full fee.

"After Georgia gained independence in 1991, Dinamo was renamed briefly as 'Iberia Tiflis' (*Dinamo has connotations with the old Soviet security regime, the KGB*), but Dinamo was such a famous name, with such a history that people realised it needed to be kept as the name."

The teenage sensation was watched by as many as could cram in as word continued to spread about this star in the making. Nobody wanted to miss the opportunity to watch potentially Georgia's first superstar and everyone wanted the opportunity to say that they watched him as a kid. Aged just 19, he scored 14 goals in 30 appearances for Dinamo in his first full season with his hometown club and played 14 times and scored 13 goals in his second season.

"At the youth tournament lots of people came to watch him," said Shota. But with Georgia often no more than a war zone, in 1993 Dinamo sent their promising young stars abroad for safety reasons. "Georgi went on loan at Saarbrucken in Germany. A lot of Georgian players had gone abroad for six months on loan back then, but we all promised to come back to Georgia after that to help the new Georgian league.

"We started in the national team together. We both made our debuts against Azerbaijan and we won 5-2, and he provided the assist for my first goal, then scored one himself. We were already very good friends by then."

After a largely unhappy time in Germany with Saarbrucken, where he made 11 starts without scoring, he returned home to resume his career. It was a tough, uncompromising league and he didn't particularly enjoy being in Germany or being away from his family. As the civil war raged on in Georgia, Kinkladze returned to the Georgian league but Dinamo president Merab Jordania wasn't prepared to risk his precocious talent in such dangerous surrounds and instead sent Georgi off to Spain. He first went to Atletico Madrid, whom it is believed were offered Georgi's talents for just £200,000 – and then Real Madrid's second team where he trained along side Raul and Morientes and more than held his own amongst the elite of club football.

During training at Real, a representative who was visiting from Boca Juniors noticed the young Georgian and shortly after they took him to Argentina for a short time. It was an amazing time for Georgi and he was thrilled when he met his hero Diego Maradona during his time at Boca. During his stay, it is believed that arguably the greatest footballer of all-time invited Georgi out for a meal. Maradona was always the player he most admired, so it was an amazing experience for him. Maradona was believed to be keen to take him to another club he was involved with in Argentina at the time but nothing transpired. Maradona, however, never forget the young midfielder from Tbilisi.

"Boca Juniors were interested, but for Georgi it was too far away from home, especially as he was so young," recalled Georgi's sister Marina.

During his stay with the Argentineans, Boca Coach Silvio Marzolini ran the rule over his European trialist but after a week or two he decided to let him return to Georgia because he felt he already was well served in that particular midfield role. Boca's playmaker was Alberto Marcico and though Marzolini felt Kinkladze was a good prospect, he felt the pair were too similar and decided that Marcico had the edge and the experience over Kinkladze. Marcico was an idol in Boca, had been an idol in Ferro Carril Oeste and even had become famous when he played in France. In short, Boca were never going to sign an unknown quantity ahead of such a hero – there would be riots on the streets.

Local journalist Ariel Cukierkorn from the *Clarin* newspaper remembered when Kinkladze arrived at Boca back in 1994. During the trial period, Kinkladze played a game for Boca in the Premier Division, against Lanus and Boca drew or lost – he is unclear about the result. Shortly after, a Boca supporter said to him: "Marzolini doesn't know anything about football because he left Kinkladze out of the team and left Marcico in who is too slow!" Cukierkorn recalled asking a board member about Kinkladze some time after he'd gone back to Georgia to which he replied: "The only thing that I can tell is that we let him go and now he is having success all over Europe," before sighing and shrugging his shoulders. As Georgi flew back home, he must have wondered where his future lay if living in Tbilisi was too dangerous. He couldn't continue to be loaned out to clubs around the globe and all he really wanted to do at that time was play for his boyhood idols Dinamo. His experiences in Europe and South America had broadened his horizons and on his return he had his best ever season with the Georgian champions, scoring 16 goals in just 24 games. As he was voted Player of the Season yet again, those watching him win match after match for Dinamo knew the gifted young star was ready for a much bigger stage.

Moves were already afoot to present him with just such an opportunity.

Chapter 3
RED TAPED

"Bloody hell, he can play! He's unbelievable. He'll have them swinging off the bloody rafters."

– Alan Ball

Kinkladze had attracted the interest of some of Europe's biggest clubs during what would be his final season with Dinamo Tbilisi. Aged 21 and with a host of top class international displays behind him, the world was his oyster.

His club form was fantastic with a terrific number of goals and assists from his central midfield position further enhancing his reputation. Yet, strangely, no club had actually placed a firm bid for his services. His time abroad with Saarbrucken and Boca Juniors had failed to yield a move away from Georgia and even trials with the Madrid giants had still ended with him returning to Tbilisi.

There was interest from several of the leading Italian clubs, particularly AC Milan, and he even earned the nickname "Rivera of the Black Sea" amongst the Italian Press. For the record, Gianni Rivera is regarded as AC Milan's greatest ever player and was the Golden Boy of Italian football during the 1960s. Highly regarded for his 'inimitable midfield leadership, ball distribution skills and sublime passes which resulted in many goals, generally scored by others from his vision' – according to Forza Azzurri website – with his one flaw was considered to be a lack of defensive skills.

Despite the comparison to the revered Rivera, it was following an awesome display against Moldova for the national team that was ultimately to be his ticket to ride, as footage of that game eventually found its way into the possession of new Manchester City chairman Francis Lee. Excited by what he'd he seen, he opened a dialogue with Dinamo Tblisi president Merab Jordania and was promised first refusal should Kinkladze ever become available. In securing Jordania's word that City would get first refusal on the player, Lee, only a few months into his tenure at the helm of the Blues, did the best bit of business he would ever do for the club.

Kinkladze's exploits against Wales, both in Georgia and Cardiff, had introduced his name to a whole host of scouts who didn't take long to decide that they were watching a special – and as yet still unsigned – talent during those games. But none had the agreement in place that Francis Lee had arranged and to the Blues' chairman's eternal credit, his foresight and timing was impeccable.

Neville Southall, record cap holder for Wales remembers the damage Kinky did against his country in the two European Championship qualifying matches in Georgia - and later Cardiff - all too well having been in goal for both matches.

"He ripped us apart in Georgia," said Southall now with Canvey Island. "He was different class and the best player on the pitch by mile. We had no information about Georgia before the game but we knew they'd be fairly decent because most Eastern Bloc teams have a lot of technical ability.

"But they murdered us in Tbilisi and we got away with a 5-0 defeat – I say got away because it could have been many, many more. Everything went through Kinkladze that day and he was just as good in the return game in Wales."

The first game in Tbilisi against the Welsh had been Georgia's record win up to that point and Kinkladze scored his first ever international goal in the 41st minute to make it 2-0. He would save his second goal for his country for the return match, some seven months later in June 1995. The quality of that second strike would also cause a frantic battle from Europe's top clubs to snap him up.

With City and a whole host of Premiership clubs well represented at Cardiff Arms Park, Kinkladze, who had been superb all evening, made for goal with not long left on the clock. He looked up and then sent a beautiful 20-yard chip sailing over Southall for the only goal of the game.

"It seemed much closer than 20 yards out," joked Southall. "I recall booting one of the Georgians as they retrieved the ball out of the net but I don't think it was Kinkladze. Around that time, it seemed that every international team had one really outstanding player. There was Hristo Stoickov at Bulgaria and many others around Europe but Kinkladze was Georgia's outstanding talent."

Southall left the pitch with the rest of the Welsh side and the disappointment in the dressing room was sprinkled with respect for the Georgians but particularly Kinkladze, who hard-nosed midfielder Barry Horne declared at the time was "the best player I've ever seen."

If Franny Lee watched that game with a big smile and a large glass of champagne at his side, who could have blamed him? While other scouts hurriedly made phone calls and typed up glowing reports about Kinkladze, he must have felt like the cat that had got the cream. A quick phone call set the wheels in motion that would end with the player leaving Georgia for good and making a new life in the English Premiership with Manchester City.

"I'd seen Kinkladze playing for Georgia in a TV clip against Wales in the European Championships qualifier in Tbilisi," recalled Lee. "I thought 'Crikey, he's exceptional' so I then called an agent – Jerome

Anderson in London – and asked if he had a complete tape of that game. He managed to get hold of one for me but the quality was bloody horrible – I've still got it, in fact – and there was a Georgian commentary as well, but you could still see the lad had brilliant ability.

"For the return match with Wales in Cardiff, I sent Jimmy Frizzell down to take a look at him and he came back and said that he thought he was quite a player: 'If you've got an orchestra, he'll conduct it,' was how he put it."

As with most deals passing through Maine Road at that time, City club secretary Bernard Halford was at the hub of the Kinkladze transfer from Dinamo from start to finish. With the impressive references from City legend Colin Bell and former manager Frizzell confirming the need to move quickly, a fee was agreed between the clubs and, true to his word, Tbilisi President Merab Jordania had given the Blues first refusal on the player.

Though Halford was aware of Kinkladze's growing reputation and the possibility he may be joining City, he didn't know how far down the line negotiations actually were between Jordania and Lee until he discovered a secret rendezvous was imminent in Zurich.

"It was the summer of 1995," recalled Halford. "Several of our scouts had watched Gio and conversations must have gone on between them and Francis. We'd had tapes of Gio in action that had been viewed throughout the summer and the deal gathered momentum when his agent, Jerome Anderson became involved after the club had decided to sign the player.

"Myself and Francis then held a secret meeting with the President of Dinamo, Merab Jordania, who was a former international player himself, and we were determined to come away with a deal in place.

"We met in a hotel room at the Zurich Hilton with Jordania and the agent and we struck a deal there and then to sign him. We'd only gone out for the day and after completing the transfer we flew back to Manchester, arriving home in the evening.

"Then, of course we had to deal with the player and settle his contract, which we did, and he flew over to England to officially sign. 'Gio' as he said he liked to be called, didn't speak any English at this point. We were having a Press conference to announce that Alan Ball was the new manager and we then told the media we had something else to announce after that.

"For once, none of the assembled journalists didn't know what it was. Alan Ball had been told about the player's imminent arrival and was perfectly happy with the situation and following the announcement of the manager, we then held another Press conference. At about 4.30pm we brought Gio in and revealed he was signing for City. It was quite a coup for the club.

"We had interpreters there to translate on his behalf and everything went well. It was quite close to the start of the season so there had been no time for anyone to see him in action but after a few training sessions it was clear to see his was a special talent.

"Tbilisi were sorry to see him go but there was a lot of poverty in Georgia at the time so this was a fantastic deal for them and the player. Gio had to move on to further his career and it was a great day for Georgian football.

"We knew what the fee was going to be – £2million – and all we had to do was agree the method of payment; instalments and so on," said Halford. "He stayed initially in a hotel but we soon found him a house near the Summerfields estate in Wilmslow and Francis spent a lot of time helping the player settle in.

"It wasn't easy for Gio at first because of the language barrier but he had English lessons as often as possible but like anything else, everyone learns at their own pace and it took Gio a while to get to grips with speaking English."

"We were also very conscious of where he had come from and the background he'd had in Georgia and the different lifestyle he was going to have in England. Obviously, it's a better standard of living here and there are more things to do and attractions that can take players' focus away, so we had people keeping an eye on him all the time so we knew where he was and what he was doing.

"We did this because we wanted to protect him so he didn't get led astray and into situations that would be difficult to handle and he wouldn't be used to and it worked quite well."

The deal between Tbilisi and City had gone very smoothly but there were still several rolls of bureaucratic tape to unravel before Kinkladze could play alongside his new teammates. It wasn't only a big deal for Manchester – the whole of Georgia had followed the transfer and Gio's sister, now known as Marina Bekeria through marriage, confirmed as much.

"When he moved to England, it was virtually unprecedented," she said. "I think Andrei Kanchelskis was the only other player from the former Soviet Union who had moved to England. Gio, of course, was the first ever Georgian. So it was a huge deal, not just for the family, but for the whole city of Tbilisi – a very proud moment."

It wasn't just Gio's family who was proud to see him playing in England. His friends and admirers were also very happy for him and for Georgian football in general, whose profile was about to reach unprecedented levels.

"Kinky's transfer to City was the biggest in the history of the former Soviet Union, so of course it was a huge thing," said close friend Shota Averladze. "He wasn't the first player to move abroad, but he was the first to move directly to one of the big leagues – I am not counting Russia. The first ever player to move abroad was Khakhadze who went to Sweden and Shengelia followed him."

The whole deal had been done without the involvement of a manager following City's failure to replace Brian Horton, sacked the previous May. In fact, the first time Alan Ball, the man chosen by Lee to lead the Blues into the next campaign saw Kinkladze in the flesh, was at the Press conference to unveil him as the new manager of the club! Ball would later claim in his autobiography that he was asked to approve the deal but the contracts had been signed before he took the Maine Road hot seat. Kinkladze was coming to play for the club anyway.

So it was that on July 15, 1995, Georgiou Kinkladze became a Manchester City player. The fee had gone up £1.8million from the £200,000 Atletico were allegedly offered to purchase Kinkladze's services less than two years' earlier but the deal still represented excellent business.

A 40-minute delay at Manchester Airport had led to the Ball Press conference going on another three hours as officials at Maine Road nervously awaited the player's arrival. Franny Lee explained that the then 14-times capped Georgian could speak little English but would soon be talking with his feet.

"He is a marvellous player," he told the assembled journalists. "We have been tracking him for six months. We asked for first option on him and his club kept their word. He could prove to become one of the best players to come out of Eastern Europe."

In a fuller interview for the *Manchester Evening News*, Lee revealed more details reporter Paul Hince.

"I watched him three times and I thought he was fantastic," said Lee. "I contacted the Tbilisi President Merab Jordania both by fax and telephone and asked if we could have first option if they ever decided to sell, which he agreed to do.

"I was worried that we might miss out on him after his performances for Georgia against Wales in the European Championships were shown around the world on TV.

"Suddenly everyone was raving about him. Tbilisi had enquiries from the likes of AC Milan and Barcelona and a lot of clubs in this country wanted to sign him – including one not so very far from Maine Road, I believe.

"But the Tbilisi President is an honourable man. He kept his word and gave us first option and I am thrilled Georgi has signed for us because he is a wonderful young player who will delight our supporters."

Jordania, who travelled over to Manchester with Kinkladze to finalise the deal, was equally fulsome in his praise for the player.

"We have produced some great players and some great teams over the years," he said at the time. "But it is my opinion that Georgiou is the best footballer ever produced by our country and is potentially the best player ever to ever come to England from the countries in the Eastern Bloc."

Agent Jerome Anderson, with his cut of the deal safely banked, dothed his cap in the direction of chairman Lee as he revealed the calibre of opposition City had fought off to secure Kinkladze's signature.

"Francis Lee beat off some of the toughest competition in the business to land his man," said Anderson. "Real Madrid, Juventus and Barcelona were just some of the big clubs waiting to have a chance to get him."

All of which went to prove how highly Kinkladze was rated around Europe and what a coup the club had pulled off. It also must have led to a few head shakes at the Bernabeu Stadium where Real could have had Kinkladze for peanuts whilst he trained with them. For Ball, however, it must have been a bit strange with Kinkladze being credited as his first signing. At Southampton, Ball's previous club, he'd worked with the irrepressible talents of Matthew Le Tissier and had known how to get the very best out of a player often – and harshly – accused of being "lazy". In many ways, he was the perfect man to manage Kinkladze and he would soon come to realise what a gem he had in his charge.

With just nine days before City set off to begin their pre-season tour of Ireland, Ball had to get to know all of his squad pretty quickly if he was to have any chance of beginning the new season on any sort of firm basis. Francis Lee remembers how he first broke the news to Ball about the Georgian's arrival.

"Alan Ball had just arrived as our new manager," said Lee, "and I said 'I've got you a good present for coming to City,' – he probably thought I'd bought a case of champagne or something like that – but then I told him we had a Georgian player coming. I added that he wasn't very big but he was the best footballer I'd ever seen.

Bally said he'd wait and see.

"Of course, after two or three training sessions he said to me 'Bloody hell, he *can* play! He's unbelievable. He'll have them swinging off the bloody rafters.' Georgi was coming anyway and we'd already signed him before Alan arrived."

Ball's now almost legendary first training session with the City squad at Platt Lane is believed to have alienated many of the City players within a few minutes by proceeding to letting them know about his own personal achievements in the game and what he expected of them. Ball then gave Kinkladze 'compassionate leave' to mentally adjust the idea of playing and living in another country.

The culture shock of moving to Manchester and leaving behind his family and friends might well have adversely affected the players' form and Ball reckoned 10 days with his former Tbilisi team-mates would enable him to hone his sharpness in familiar surrounds and allow him to come to terms with the transfer.

It was a subtle and clever move on Ball's part, but it also effectively ruled Kinkladze out of the Irish tour.

"He sees himself as the flag bearer of Georgia and a pioneer for his countrymen. It was all a bit too much too soon for the lad," said Ball at the time. "It will be more beneficial for him to train with his old teammates before returning to us.

"I've got a month to bed him in. The hurly burly of our league will be a big test for him. He may not speak much English but he speaks the language of the game."

So with Kinkladze back in Georgia, Ball took his squad to Galway for the first of the pre-season friendly matches. Back in Manchester, a storm was brewing. Somewhere along the line, the small matter of a work permit for Kinkladze had been overlooked and it seemed likely he would now miss the start of the season. The confusion was compounded by the Blues' managing director Colin Barlow, who commented that as far as he was concerned, there wasn't a problem, but added: "I can't say categorically we have applied for a work permit."

There didn't seem to be any panic at Maine Road and Barlow also claimed that the club had been taking advice from PFA boss Gordon Taylor about the situation and he'd said 'there would be no problem'. Of course, the tabloids lapped it up. In their eyes, here was Dear Old City bumbling along as usual, entertaining the masses on and off the park. Paul Walker in *The Star* claimed the player was "stranded in Moscow, having to queue up with others at the British Embassy waiting to be issued a visa."

The visa didn't appear and Kinkladze had to spend the night in a Moscow hotel while City desperately tried to tie things up at their end, which included obtaining proof of the players' international appearances. Days passed and Ball must have wondered when he would get the opportunity to watch his new signing in action during a match with the big kick-off now just days away. The City fans, too, awaited their first glimpse of the player they had heard so much about of late but seen so little, to make his bow.

The tour of Ireland had gone well with a 3-0 win over Galway United and a 2-0 win over Cork City and the encouraging form continued with a 1-0 at Stockport County, but those would be the only victories in the seven-match build up to the start of the season.

A 2-1 loss at Wolves was followed by a worrying 2-1 defeat to Burnley and the sizeable City followings at each game returned home with their preconceived fears that Ball was the wrong choice as manager growing by the game. A little unfair, perhaps, so early into his career at Maine Road but his appointment had been greeted by more grudging acceptance rather than anything else. His track record as a boss just didn't excite supporters.

Ball's need to get Kinkladze in his starting eleven for the mini-tour of Scotland was increasing by the day. With two days to go before the clash with Raith Rovers, news broke of the proof the Department of Employment were demanding for the internationals played by the club's only summer signing and the likelihood that he would make his debut north of the border began to recede.

City ploughed on with the same squad that finished the previous season poorly and a 2-2 draw at Raith was followed two days later by a disastrous 5-1 hammering at Hearts, but the mini-crisis of faith was about to be eased. For Ball, there was at last a silver lining to the appalling pre-season form. Confirmation was received that Kinkladze's work permit would be issued in time for him to make his debut a week later in the opening Premiership match of the season. Ball was hugely relieved and the supporters could at last look forward to their first look at a player they had already heard so much about.

Kinkladze flew into Manchester to finally begin his City career and train with his new teammates. The story attracted a few column inches in the nationals, overshadowed by the arrivals of Ruud Guillit at Chelsea and Dennis Bergkamp at Arsenal. Ball, having now watched his protégé in action a couple of times on the Platt Lane training pitches was happy the attention was diverted elsewhere.

"I'm delighted nobody has put pressure on him and picked him out," he commented in the week leading up to the Spurs game. "His football will do the talking. I don't want to put the kiss of death on him but if I've ever seen top talent, this is it."

From the man who had Matt Le Tissier in his charge for several seasons, this was quite a compliment. Meanwhile, Franny Lee was ensuring that all was well off the pitch for the young newcomer. He wondered how it might feel to be thousands of miles from home and decided to look out for Gio from day one.

"When he came over to stay, we had an interpreter for him because he couldn't speak one word of English," recalled Lee. "It was a major problem. We put him in the Mottram Hall Hotel and the agent went back to London and his Ukrainian interpreter went home, too and I walked out of the hotel myself and stopped and thought 'Christ! What's it going to be like for that poor kid, now?' I'd told the staff to look after him and if he needed anything they were to give me a call at home and I'd come and see if everything was okay.

"I thought of how I'd feel myself if I'd just signed for a club in Russia and was stuck in a hotel on my own and couldn't speak the language – I knew I'd be struggling and alone. So we tried to make him feel at home and I got everybody including Gary, my son, to spend a lot of time with him and make him feel wanted and welcome. At first the hotel staff told me that he didn't eat very well. I thought that was perhaps down to a change of environment and a different culture but he never ate anything that could be fattening and never drank alcohol and never smoked. He didn't go out with women in those days… I don't know how he ever made it as a footballer!"

Over the coming months, however, Gio would prove that he was focused only on one thing - playing football and he soon settled into Manchester life, thanks largely to the Lee family. But by the time he was due to walk down the tunnel for his Manchester City debut, he was on his own again and he would be expected to produce the goods.

Chapter 4

SEVEN UP

"We went to Kinky's first game and came away thinking, 'Well, we're either going to win the European Cup or we'll be in the Fourth Division in five years."

– Noel Gallagher

Searing heat, not something most Mancunians are used to, greeted the 22 Manchester City and Tottenham players as they strode out to 'Roll With It' by Oasis. It was August 19, 1995. The Maine Road turf, resplendent in the late summer sunshine and in its customary tip-top condition after being lovingly tendered by groundsman Stan Gibson during the close season, was lush and green and ready for football to be played upon it.

The terraces long gone, the all-seater crowd of 30,827 settled into their seats after cheering the Blues' players as the announcer called each name out and various pleasantries were exchanged with the Tottenham fans as the minutes ticked towards three o'clock.

The stragglers from the bars jostled for their place amongst shouts of 'sit down!' as referee Graham Poll strolled to the centre circle in preparation and the air of anticipation was as tangible as ever. Pre-match chat buzzed around the stadium and old acquaintances, that only seem to meet up on matchdays, shared the usual mix of pessimism, optimism, small talk and banter.

Alan Ball had seen enough in the pre-season friendlies to know his squad needed re-enforcements and had snapped up German goalkeeper, Eike Immel and Portsmouth's highly rated centre back, Kit Symons in time for the opening game. Of course, there was also the relatively unknown quantity from Georgia, Georgiou Kinkladze who had at least enjoyed a week's training with the squad, even if he'd not played competitively with them.

Former City manager Tony Book was now on the backroom staff at Maine Road and he remembered watching Kinkladze train, saying he was 'magnificent to watch – absolutely brilliant'. Kinkladze wore the No.7 shirt for his first appearance for the club and, donning one of the best looking City strips of recent times – sky blue jersey, with white shorts and white socks – the chunky midfielder certainly looked the part prior to kick-off. He even looked a little embarrassed as the supporters cheered his name and applauded him when he was first introduced.

Within minutes of the kick-off, the Georgian international had played a couple of sweet passes and one delicious, nonchalant flick with the outside of his boot. He had immediately captivated the home support with an audible air of expectancy beginning to rise from the crowd each time the ball was played to him.

This was to become the norm for the next 36 months, though nobody could have predicted quite how strong the bond would become between player and the fans or how dangerously dependent the team would become on his razor sharp football brain. Applause and appreciative murmurs greeted every pass, dummy or shake of the hips and his ability to make an opponent look a mug was lapped up with enthusiasm.

But City being City, it was Spurs who opened the scoring with a Teddy Sheringham header on 33 minutes and that remained the score until the break. Half-time chatter was generally centred on Kinkladze, with the wiser heads not completely sold on the new star. The Blues came out and equalised six minutes into the second half to secure a point and everyone went home satisfied. Kinkladze had done more than enough on his debut to feel satisfied with himself. Nicky Summerbee would become Gio's best pal during his time at Maine Road and he recalled the Georgian's early days at Maine Road.

"When he first came over he couldn't speak a word of English but we seemed to hit it off as mates," said Summerbee. "We'd go out and he wouldn't speak much – it was a bit odd because it was just the two of us but there must have been some sort of friendship there at the beginning. On the pitch, too, when he did pick up the language, we got on well and we used to go out regularly.

"When you really got to know Georgi, he had a really good sense of humour – very sarcastic – he was funny but people wouldn't really see that side of his personality, but believe me, he could cut you down as well as anyone else.

"I think when he first came nobody knew much about him so there was no pressure on him to peform, but as soon as the fans saw what he could do, they more or less liked him straight away. As players, we knew how good he was because we obviously trained with him every day. He was an exceptional talent."

Much of the radio phone-in chatter after the Spurs match was about Kinkladze with many reckoning the club had found a special footballer; somebody who could get people out of their seats with a disguised pass or the ability to almost dance around opponents. Whatever shortcomings there was the opening day performance by the Blues was glossed over and the opinion was that Gio was a star in the making.

Paul Hince, City correspondent on the *Manchester Evening News* began his own personal Kinkladze fan club in the Monday edition match report.

"And what a gem the Blues have unearthed in little Kinkladze", wrote Hince. "Ball's first match as manager is likely to be the day a star was born with the big Maine Road crowd drooling at "Kinky's" gorgeous touch and his ability to leave opponents for dead with just a shimmy of his hips."

Hince marked Ian Brightwell as man of the match with nine out ten but gave the newly christened 'Kinky' eight. Alan Ball, clearly relieved that things had gone reasonably well was prepared to build the team around this prestigious new talent and he was quick to pile the praise on the 22 year-old. After lauding Brightwell and Kit Symons' display in the centre of defence, Ball said:

"And what can I say about our other new boy Georgi Kinkladze? I think the City supporters saw a rare talent playing his first match in this country. He is like Matt Le Tissier in that you give him the ball in the right situations and he will punish the opposition. I have been telling anyone who cared to listen that Kinky will have the fans flocking to see him this season and perhaps now you will begin to see what I mean."

The expectancy levels were already in place. It had been quite a debut.

City next travelled to Highfield Road four days later to face Coventry City and Kinkladze was the only shining light in a disappointing 2-1 defeat and the Blues followed that up with an equally flat display in a 1-0 loss at QPR. The strain on Kinkladze's face, now generally known to one and all fans as 'Kinky', was even greater as Ball's confusing tactics saw Everton leave Maine Road with all three points four days later with a 2-0 win.

The Toffees, managed by former City hero Joe Royle, bagged two second half goals and Royle popped his head around the office of his former team-mate Tony Book, now Youth Team Coach at Maine Road and said: "Kinkladze's a great talent, Booky… but he'll get you all the sack." Considering what the future held in store for Royle, those words would take on extra resonance in future years.

The little Georgian must have wondered what he'd let himself in for as his new team continued their miserable start to the campaign. More worryingly for chairman Francis Lee was the attendance for the next game; a Sunday live televised clash with Arsenal. Just under 24,000 turned up for a game that the Blues huffed and puffed and for almost 90 minutes, seemed set to take a morale boosting point from until Ian Wright, whose two young sons Shaun and Bradley would eventually play for City, popped up with a last second goal to win the game and dump to the bottom of the table.

While Ball bemoaned referee Dermot Gallagher had cost his side a point, the supporters drifted home wondering when, if ever, the first victory would come along. How Kinky must have wished he could have been part of the next team he faced, Newcastle United, as Kevin Keegan's slick, free-flowing attack minded outfit proceeded to tear the Blues apart at St James' Park.

Only Eike Immel prevented a massacre as the Geordies won 3-1 and further cut adrift City at the foot of the table. One thing was becoming clear already – if Kinky had an off day or the game largely passed him by, the Blues had little to offer in terms of attack or invention. The papers, as ever, cranked up the media doom machine and question marks already hung heavily over the future of Ball in many of the nationals.

Worse was to come as City drew 0-0 with Division Three strugglers Wycombe Wanderers in the Coca-Cola Cup and then were soundly beaten at Nottingham Forest by three goals to nil and then lost again, this time by the only goal of the game at home to Middlesbrough. Nine games into his City career and Gio was still yet to taste victory in his new club's colours. His skills, which appeared in flashes here and there, were the only highlight of what was a desperate start to the season – City's worst ever in the top-flight, in fact.

Then, not taking into account the quality of the opposition, the dark cloud briefly lifted as City saw off Wycombe 4-0 with Kinky's sublime through ball for Uwe Rosler's second goal and his jinking run that ended with a penalty, at last enabling him to leave the pitch with a smile on his face. Ball later remarked that it was a pity only 11,474 fans were there to witness the victory but considering the football that had been served up prior to that fixture, he was perhaps lucky that anyone turned up on the night! It was also, incidentally, one of the highest gates of the evening.

Gio's much-hyped first Manchester derby ended in defeat and a goalless draw with Leeds continued the miserable form in the league but if things had been bad, they were about to get even worse and the four days between October 25 and October 28 were about to test the patience of supporters to very limit. City's 'reward' for beating Wycombe was a trip to Anfield, where, ironically, the Blues would play again in the Premiership the following Saturday.

Imagine the excitement felt by Kinky as he first stepped out on the turf of the team he used to imagine himself playing for when he was a small boy back in Tbilisi. Here he was, running down that famous tunnel, touching the 'This is Anfield' sign before stepping out against his boyhood heroes. He warmed up glancing over at the Kop, within touching distance, for the very first time. Of course, the Blues were going to lose the game as they generally always did at Anfield; it was just a matter of by how many. Four without reply was the answer, including one from 21 year-old striker Robbie Fowler, as Gio's dream fixture quickly turned sour. City's next visit, a couple of days later, ended even more disastrously, as they were hammered 6–0 by the Reds. Things were getting worse and it was hard to imagine Ball seeing the week out as radio phone-ins were jammed with calls from disgruntled Blues whilst red-tops speculated just how long Lee could allow things to continue. It had been a calamitous few days and the pressure on Ball and the team was at almost unsustainable levels.

Two points from 33 threatened City not only with relegation, but the lowest points tally ever in the top division if things continued unabated. It was a pity that the Blues had a gem of a player in their midfield but he was becoming all-but lost in all the trauma surrounding the team, chairman and manager. What odds, then, of Ball being awarded the manager of the month just four weeks later? Let's remember this is Manchester City, where what will be will probably not quite be the way it is supposed to and the incredible often rubs shoulders with the unbelievable.

November was not only to be the beginning of City's season; it was the month that Georgiou Kinkladze and his new teammates finally settled down, gelled and began to really produce the goods. Gio set up Nicky Summerbee's winner against Bolton Wanderers for the first victory and he again sparkled in the 1-1 draw at Sheffield Wednesday, finally moving City off the bottom, even though they'd only collected six points in total.

A hard fought last minute win against Wimbledon moved them further away from the foot of the table but it was the next game that had the Maine Road faithful eating out of the Georgian's hand. His performance against Aston Villa was as good as many fans had ever seen a City player play and the calibre of his display was, in every sense of the word, magical.

Against a Villa side packed with talent and a defence that included the likes of Gareth Southgate, Steve Staunton, Paul McGrath and Ugo Ehiogu, Kinky tormented, dribbled and used every trick in his extensive repertoire in order to unlock the visitors' defence. Ultimately, he had to do it himself as, with minutes left, he played a wonderful one-two with Niall Quinn leaving him clear on goal to whip the ball into the net from a tight angle and send the home fans wild. He ran to the North Stand where he was duly mobbed – everyone wanted to congratulate him and he was almost lost in the melee.

Ball, understandably, couldn't contain himself in the after-match press conference and who could blame him? Teetering on the brink one minute, riding high and sticking two fingers up to the journalists who had been reading his last rites the next.

"I don't like signalling out players because this was basically a tremendous team performance," he said. "But Georgi Kinkladze was absolutely outstanding. He is only 22 and he represents the kind of future which myself and Francis Lee want for Manchester City. He is a fantastic talent."

Nobody was arguing. Kinkladze had managed to help the Blues' fans forget about the turgid opening 11 league games and his influence on the team, when he was in the mood, was electrifying. Ball ended November by being voted Manager of the Month in the kind of turnaround that can only happen to City. If you wrote their script, you'd be laughed out of town. Arguably, Kinky had saved his manager's job and it was no wonder he lifted him shoulder high as he celebrated his winner against Villa.

Of course, there was much more to come from the player who was already attracting numerous column inches as the tabloids speculated on who would be taking him away from Maine Road. The *Manchester Evening News*, meanwhile, voted Kinky their Sports Personality of the Month.

"The Manchester City fans have made it easier for me to live in a new environment," said Georgi, speaking through an interpreter, shortly after he'd been presented with the award. "It was strange for me to come to a new country and it did not help when we had such a bad start. But the fans did not react as they might back home. They do not whistle players over mistakes - not even when a penalty is given away.

"They accept things and concentrate on encouraging their team. There are no recriminations. I felt a little lonely and afraid after my first game but these feelings soon went, thanks to the supporters."

The difficult start to life in England paled into insignificance when compared with some of Gio's experiences in Georgia, as he was about to reveal...

Chapter 5
GEORGI BEST

"I feel Manchester is my second home because of the chairman, the manager, my teammates and the Manchester people. I feel like I was born here."

– Georgi Kinkladze

From the more salubrious surrounds of Georgi's new Wilmslow home, the family-orientated star recalled his upbringing in Georgia, when the country was still fighting for its independence from the Soviet Union. It was a time of bullets and cold-blooded murder that saw many friends hurt and former colleagues killed. A small but fiercely proud people, Georgia has never been very far from his heart.

"It is still difficult to discuss because so many friends have died for no reason," he stated in December 1995. "The war affected everybody in Georgia. We couldn't go out in the evening because we were afraid of the guns people carried. Somebody could be killed by accident. Lots of friends were badly affected and two of my old club managers died. They were just driving when somebody shot them."

Questions about whether he was happy in England and whether or not he regretted moving to City were asked and Georgi admitted things had not gone as he'd hoped since his debut against Spurs.

"I'm happy to be here in Manchester," he said. "I like it, but my heart is in Georgia and I'm thinking about my country and people all the time. I'm so proud every time I play football for my country. The first few months at City have been difficult and I did wonder if

I had made a big mistake. I know Real Madrid were interested and I have also spent some time in Germany and Argentina."

Gio also revealed, for the first time, details of his time before Maine Road and his early days in Georgia.

"When I was a boy, I loved watching Liverpool and other English teams and that is why it was my dream to play in the Premiership. I was always mad on football as a child and I was with the Dinamo Tbilisi youth team from the age of seven.

"But my mother wanted me to be a folk dancer so when my father went to work in Russia for three years, she hid away my football boots and took me to dancing classes."

Talk of his mother, Khatuna, clearly moved the player who, at the time, had not seen his family for several months. City were doing their utmost to get her over for his first Christmas in England but the British Embassy twice refused her an entry visa. At least he had the company of interpreter Natalie Jordania, daughter of Tbilisi president Merab during those lonely first few months.

The Georgian star had also attracted the interest of several self-styled 'advisers'. Turkish-born Roberto Ferraro claimed to have become close to Gio's and announced he was his "friend, big brother and father figure". He had even claimed credit for the stunning goal against Aston Villa after advising Kinky not to eat after 4pm, 48 hours before a match. Bizarrely, Ferraro claimed to have found this nugget of wisdom on TV. "I got that from a programme about South American footballers," he said. "That's what Maradona does," he added. Unfortunately, Maradona was also using several other ways of suppressing his hunger around that time and Ferraro's involvement was a little unorthodox to say the least but presumably Gio wouldn't have given him the time of day if he wasn't happy with his comments or his company.

Ferraro also took it upon himself to inform the media that Kinky loved Orange Tango, crispy pizza, Chinese food and McDonalds – the latter being his favourite after-match meal. Whether he took any notice of the Turk's advice on diets or not, Gio was still inspiring the resurgent Blues to a 1-0 at Leeds.

Franny Lee was as excited as anyone by his protégé's form and was relieved that things had at last started to go his way. How many talented imports have not weathered the storm, ended up playing reserve football and then been on the first plane back home? City have had a few themselves, down the years.

"As soon as the team started to play, he was exceptional, wasn't he?" said Lee. "I remember the time we beat Leeds 1-0 away in November 1995 and Gary McCallister, who I see quite a lot of these days, was playing. Gary said 'I'll never forget that day. He turned me one way; he turned me the other way and I turned back and nearly screwed myself into the ground! I hadn't a clue what he was doing and he just made me look a complete monkey.' McAllister's manager told him to mark Kinkladze closer and he said that was the last thing he wanted to do!"

The media then enthused over one of the imminent midfield clashes of the season. Middlesbrough v Manchester City may not seem like a game the national press and many in football couldn't wait to see, but the fact that Boro's own midfield darling Juninho was pitting his wits against Gio Kinkladze, made this an entirely different proposition. Speculation had raged as to who was the greater talent – Juninho was established at the Riverside and was a great favourite with the Boro supporters whilst Kinkladze was the new kid on the block. Most clubs would have gladly accommodated either star in their side at the time.

City, on the back of a terrific unbeaten run of five games began with some beautiful football and, on 16 minutes, the Blues' Georgian maestro struck a wonderful solo goal. He received the ball from a Brightwell throw-in just inside the Boro half, and then wandered into the centre of the park before turning sharply towards goal leaving two Boro midfielders in his wake. He then ghosted past another challenge 25 yards out, sold a dummy to two defenders just inside the box and then placed a shot accurately in at the far post with his left foot, just out of the reach of goalkeeper Gary Walsh. The travelling Blues support went crazy. Here was their own potential superstar upstaging Boro's Brazilian hero in his own backyard. The game was set for a battle of wits between two tremendous talents but despite Kinky's best efforts, Boro raised their game to run out 4-1 winners and the wonder goal was quickly forgotten. Most agreed the two stars were unique talents but the general consensus was, despite being on the losing team, Kinkladze's was the greater. The Middlesbrough fans didn't forget Kinkladze's performance that day and voted him 'best opposing player' at the end of the season.

At least the new version of Oasis' 'Wonderwall' was given an airing by the travelling army at the Riverside. Subtle lyric changes resulted in the following:

"And all the runs that Kinky makes are winding,

And all the goals that City score are blinding,

There are many things that I, would like to say to you but I don't know how,

'Cos maybe, you're gonna be the one that saves me,

And after all,

You're my Alan Ball."

The Oasis connection at City was reaching fever pitch around this time with Maine Road concerts announced for the following summer and both the band and the club keen to exploit the connection – and branding opportunities - to the full. City's shirt was worn by hundreds of Oasis fans that had never been within 50 miles of Maine Road and team continued to run out to 'Roll With It' before home fixtures were played. Oasis were undoubtedly the biggest British band for a decade and City fans were more than happy with the cross-referencing. They had the biggest and best rock band in the world - according to Noel Gallagher – as fans; the most fashionable kit in the Premiership and one of the most gifted players in the world in Georgi Kinkladze.

Meanwhile, away from football, Gio had received the best possible personal news he could have wished for when it was announced his mother would be travelling to Manchester to spend the rest of the season at his home in Cheshire and, more importantly, be there to celebrate her son's first Christmas away from Georgia. Gio greeted the news with delight.

"I am very happy," he told reporters. "Of course, with all the problems in my homeland I have been worried about my family and have missed my mother. I am proud of my country and family and have felt homesick at times this season. It is good that she is finally here."

Khatuna Kinkladze arrived with a bulging suitcase full of her only son's favourite foods, including chicken in walnut sauce, baked bread and cheese and walnut puddings covered in dried grape juice. Presumably, Roberto Ferraro's 48-hour diet was quickly confined to the dustbin around this time! Gio's mum said that she was very happy that her son had found fame in another country and she was happy to be able to come and look after him. "I'm his mother and that's what mothers are for," she added.

It was another chance for the national media to get their fix of Kinkladze into the back pages. There was a fascination and respect that, for now, rendered him almost untouchable at the time, but this, as it surely had to, would change for the worse in the years ahead. The media in general and supporters of every club in the country, most of whom had never seen such individual skill on English soil up to that point, admired him from afar and it seemed and negative stories just wouldn't wash at this time.

Back on the pitch, City ended the year without a win in their next three games and the spectre of relegation, never far from anyone's minds connected with the club, re-emerged with vengeance. Opposing teams were getting wise to Kinkladze's ability – not that they could always do anything to stop it – legally, anyway – and were either man-marking him with a dedicated shadow during the match or placing a hatchet man on him with the intention of putting him out of the game. Two, sometimes three players were often deployed to mark him. The message was clear: stop Kinkladze and you stop City. He was having to think of new ways to outwit opponents but was routinely scythed down with the offender more than happy to accept a yellow card in the hope of seeing the Blues' No.7 limp towards the dressing room as a result. But his father's tough training regimes meant he could withstand the majority of kicks to the knee, ankles or thighs. All the various strengthening exercises Robizon had developed for his son were now paying dividends and Gio was proving a tough character, made of sterner stuff than the cynical Sunday league pub challenges he was being subjected to.

After the Blues saw off West Ham 2-1 for the opening game of 1996, he missed his first game for the club and the question that most people were already wondering was: how would City play without him? Though the Blues lacked a little imagination, a 0-0 draw in the FA Cup at First Division Leicester City answered that particular question, but while some argued that City hadn't always played well when Gio was on the pitch, most felt they were always likely to play better and had a much greater chance of winning when he was.

He was back for the replay and Leicester were soon wishing they had taken their chance to see off the Blues at Filbert Street as he inspired City to a wonderful 5-0 win, setting up three and scoring what was fast becoming an almost customary cracking solo goal. He entertained the Kippax after the break with some incredible juggling skills and left the pitch to a standing ovation and chants of "Gio! Gio! Gio!"

Yet nights such as that were still few and far between. Ball's signings were questionable to say the least and the additions of Gerry Creaney, Michael Frontzeck and Nigel Clough added no real quality to the team at all. Martin Phillips, signed from Exeter was burdened by Ball who claimed not long after the youngster arrived at Maine Road that he would be "the first £10million player."

What Gio really lacked was protection from the men sent out to cut him in half each weekend. Despite having Steve Lomas and Garry Flitcroft alongside him in the middle, nobody seemed willing to take the protective role when it came to some of the horrific challenges that were flying in. Referees, too, failed the City hero, often allowing a couple of rash tackles before eventually producing a yellow card when often a red was more deserving.

As City moved towards the back end of February, their form was still patchy but their destiny was at least still very much in their own hands. After seeing off Coventry City in the FA Cup, they travelled across the city to Old Trafford to take on Manchester United for a place in the last eight. The Blues, backed by around 8,000 fans, began brightly and Gio's deft through ball put Uwe Rosler in the clear and the German striker lobbed Peter Schmeichel from 20 yards for the opening goal. If Alex Ferguson was indeed one of the Georgian's potential suitors, as he was rumoured to be at the time, Gio had picked the right time to impress him further.

Unfortunately, referee Alan Wilkie was in charge and his diabolical handling of the game has become almost legendary amongst City fans down the years, such was his ineptness. Whether Wilkie felt guilty about being the official who sent Eric Cantona off at Crystal Palace off or not is open to debate. Cantona subsequently became embroiled with a fan on his way to way for an early bath, and then was banned for several months as a result. Perhaps he felt he owed United a favour – only he knows the answer to that particular question but it is one 8,000 Blues wanted to ask him personally at the time.

The man City fans loathe with a passion, Roy Keane, should have been sent off for one disgusting challenge alone on Kinkladze, reacted by remonstrating with Wilkie when he blew his whistle before he realised a penalty had been awarded when Frontzeck was adjudged to have fouled Cantona from a corner. It was so ludicrous it was almost funny. Almost, but not quite. It allowed United to get back on level terms and City eventually lost 2-1. Gio's boyhood dream of playing in an FA Cup final at Wembley looked as distant as ever.

Behind the scenes at Maine Road, Franny Lee was already talking with Gio about a new-improved contract to keep the player at Maine Road for longer than his current three-year deal. It was a wise move with the vultures hovering over Maine Road to pick the carcass clean should City fail to escape the relegation quagmire. Kinkladze, his English improving all the time was keeping his cards close to his chest.

"I have a three-year deal and I would like to extend it," he said. "But that will be decided between Francis Lee and myself. I have settled very well and I feel Manchester is my second home because of the chairman, the manager, my teammates and the Manchester people. I feel like I was born here."

All of this made pleasant reading for the supporters who had come to adore the Georgian but many felt much still depended on the small matter of City staying in the Premier League. It was almost obscene to think of Kinkladze playing the likes of Southend United and Grimsby Town on a regular basis but that was a distinct possibility if he committed himself to a new deal too early.

In the meantime, it was time for another clash of the Premiership's football geniuses with Keegan's Newcastle next up at Maine Road and the prospect of David Ginola in opposition to Kinky. Typically, Keegan employed none of the hatchet man-markers other managers had resorted to and allowed football to be played with a 'may the best team win' attitude. The result was a minor classic that played out in front of the *Match of the Day* cameras to an appreciative audience of millions, many of whom later added their names to the growing fan club of City's mercurial No.7.

The Ginola v Kinkladze clash did not disappoint, either. The elegant Frenchman, with an infuriating penchant for diving and making a meal of tackles rasped three shots in the opening exchanges that all nearly resulted in goals but while he was perhaps a little more selfish near goal, Kinky was definitely more of a team man, making chances for others. Maybe the key to his popularity amongst other football supporters was that while Ginola and others like him rolled around in mock agony from a variety of challenges – many that were hardly more than a good solid tackle - Kinkladze refused to join in the diving antics who were giving foreign talent a bad name, despite the regular punishment handed in his direction.

Kinky and Ginola were both on fire during the game that had everything – goals, controversy, off the ball incidents and individual brilliance, most of which was served up by the latter pair. Some of the Georgian's footwork would not have been out of place with the Royal Ballet and his days learning the Georgian folk dancing were never used to better effect and on at least three occasions he beat four men in the blink of an eye, one almost resulting in (yet another) world class goal. The game ended 3-3 but the Press, TV pundits and the rest of the country were talking about the performance of one man after the game, and he wasn't French.

Chapter 6
GEORGI FAME

"I'm running out of superlatives when I talk about him. All I can say is that his second goal, breathtaking as it was, didn't surprise me at all."

– Alan Ball

"That's mesmeric!"

Jon Champion, BBC TV

The clamour to prise Kinky away from Maine Road really began on March 16, 1996 at approximately 3.40pm. From that moment on, the Blues had to fend off all-comers determined to get the Georgian away from Moss Side with many able to offer the lure of mega wages and Champions League football.

City had slumped in form again going into March and two defeats and two draws in four games meant the fight to avoid relegation would most likely go on until the last kick of the season, unless there was some dramatic improvements out on the park. Alan Ball's former club Southampton were the visitors on a grey, wet Saturday afternoon in early spring – the kind of afternoon Mancunians barely bat an eye at – but the weather was the last thing on anyone's mind that day. Those grey clouds would have become positively black if fellow strugglers Southampton left Maine Road with all three points.

Defeat was unthinkable and the Blues, for once, came out in the mood to make sure that didn't happen. The hosts were on top from the kick-off and with 15 minutes gone, Kinkladze let fly with a scorching drive that shook every drop of water off the Platt Lane end crossbar. The Saints had been warned but they clung on until 34 minutes had been played when finally,

City's dominance paid off. Nicky Summerbee played a peach of a pass through to Nigel Clough and Dave Beasant palmed his cross-shot out into the path of Kinky who swept the ball home for the opening goal. Happy though he was, he looked almost embarrassed to have scored such a mundane effort.

With their tails up, City pressed for a second and with 40 minutes on the clock, Steve Lomas played the ball to Kinkladze, wide on the right about 35 yards from goal. He nudged the ball towards Simon Charlton and was away from him the blink of an eye. He then approached – and left – Ken Monkou for dead with a sway of the hips before nicking the ball delicately through two despairing defenders on the edge of the box. With just Beasant to beat, he waited, waited, waited… until he was almost on top of the giant keeper before nonchalantly lifting the ball over Beasant's right shoulder with that magical left peg for an unforgettable goal.

Maine Road erupted.

Those inside the famous old ground knew they'd seen something incredible and the celebrations continued for several minutes and the noise levels of people, literally awestruck, went on to half-time when the team, but especially Kinky, received an ovation saved only for very, very special occasions. That Kinkladze was a genius, nobody doubted but the sheer brilliance of very likely the best goal ever scored at Maine Road had taken everyone's breath away – if ever there was an 'I was there' moment' for City fans to treasure, this had been it. It seemed the whole crowd converged in the concourses below the stands at the break to watch the goal replayed and each time it was, it received roars of appreciation who, let's face it, weren't used to seeing such quality.

Match of the Day had chosen wisely and commentator Jon Champion declared, "That's mesmeric, that's sublime…that is Georgiou Kinkladze!" as the Georgian ran to the Platt Lane to receive his adulation. Champion, now working for ITV Sport, has never forgotten that goal or the player who scored it and even in early 2005, he could recall the precise date it all happened.

"The date was March 16, 1996 and it's indelibly etched on mind," said Champion. "It was, on paper, a run of the mill Premiership match between City and Southampton with City worried about relegation. Southampton were a very workmanlike side and the game was meandering along quite happily until Georgi's moment of brilliance. He picked the ball up on the right, just over the halfway line and right in front of our commentary position in the Main Stand gantry. I remember him picking up the ball and proceeded to go on this run that you couldn't imagine any other player embarking on. At that time, from that position a Manchester City player could and should have done anything but what Georgi Kinkladze did.

"He put his head down and went on one of those mesmeric, weaving runs around every defender and beating one or two of them twice if my memory serves me well. The that struck me the most was his hips – he had a pair of hips that could do things that human hips shouldn't be able to do in terms of deceiving defenders and I recall the likes of Ken Monkou, Richard Hall, Jason Dodd and Simon Charlton – the poor hapless back four of Southampton, the majority of whom all tried to tackle him on that run. It all happened in a blur, but looking back on it you can remember the minute details of it and then poor Dave Beasant knew that he was in trouble and was rendered the most helpless man on the pitch at that moment because once Kinkladze had beaten all those defenders there was no way he was going to fall at the final hurdle. I said it was fantastic, sublime and mesmeric and it was one of the easiest goals I've ever had to commentate on in my career, just because the wonderful, out of the ordinary moments come so easily – you just rely on the latent vocabulary in your head and allow emotion to take over.

"I would put it on a par with Michael Owen's goal in St Etienne against Argentina which I was also lucky enough to be commentating on. I remember getting to half time and still almost trembling with the excitement of what we'd all just witnessed. Maine Road was the most wonderful place to watch football because of the genuine affection of the fans towards the players and I remember looking around at the crowd and I could see people still shaking their heads as they opened flasks and slapping each other on the back as if to say, 'hey, in 20 years time we'll still be saying we were there, that day.'"

Hardly surprising then, the second half was something of an anti-climax with the Blues just about clinging on for a 2-1 win and loosening the noose around their necks a little. The Press were full of praise for City's No.7 in the Sunday papers but it wasn't only the British public who were falling under the Georgian's magical spell. A player's strike in Italy meant that there was no football that weekend and instead of Serie A highlights appearing on Italian TV, they concentrated on the Premiership and one game – or more to the point, one goal scored by Kinkladze – received special attention.

Tentative enquiries immediately began to flood in but City were adamant that the player was going nowhere. "We already have our answer ready and that's a firm 'No way'," Ball said in answer to journalists' probing questions about unwanted interest from abroad. "We knew we had signed a jewel and that's why we gave him a three-year deal," Ball added defiantly.

But since when did Italian clubs take 'no' for an answer? Juventus and AC Milan were believed to be heading the queue to make City an offer they couldn't refuse. But the Blues had their own persuasive ways and on Gio's recommendation, they opened up talks with Spartak Vladikavkaz for the services of Gio's good friend and Georgia teammate Mikhail Kavlashvili, who Kinky claimed was "better than I am." City fans held their breath!

But of course, the Italians would not be dissuaded so easily. AC Milan and Barcelona, both long-time suitors of the Georgian - even back to his days at Dinamo - were each believed to be lining up bids in excess of £7million. But with Garry Flitcroft's £3.2million move to Blackburn completed, there was no desperate need for extra cash, though the timing of the sale of such an influential battler was poor to say the least. Selling Flitcroft was undoubtedly Francis Lee's only way of financing a new, much improved deal to ensure that Kinky remained with City and the get-out clause from his original deal was papered over with what was reported to have been a £10,000 per week pay rise and a signing on fee – all unconfirmed. If that was the case, nobody argued he was worth every penny but the timing of the whole affair seemed to be somewhat skew-whiffed with the Blues entering such a critical time of the season. Lee and Ball knew they were taking a gamble and, to be fair, most City fans at that time would have probably done the same if it meant hanging on to their prized asset.

The figures and details of Kinky's new deal widely reported in the media were way off the mark, according to his agent Jerome Anderson. He claimed a new contract had indeed been signed and that his client was very happy with it: "But I can assure you it is nothing like £13,000 a week," argued Anderson.

Back where things really counted, on the pitch, Kinky was imperious as City travelled to West Ham in search of their first win on the road since the beginning of December. Kinky cut the Hammers' defence to ribbons and was a constant threat every time he had the ball but as chance after chance was spurned West Ham took the initiative and eventually ran out 4-2 winners. It was a bitter blow and one that underscored the ineptitude amongst some of the City players at the time. There was plenty of other talent within the squad and it wasn't quite a one-man team, but time after time, gilt-edged chances were being wasted and too many games that should have ended in City winning resulted in defeat.

A point at Bolton Wanderers a week later, where Kinky was subjected to the kind of roughhouse tactics that had become the norm was accompanied by a stark warning by Trotters midfielder Alan Thompson. He claimed that Kinkladze would have to get used to such treatment as opponents signalled him out as the man that made the Blues tick. "He's every bit the player people say he is," said Thompson. "But Kinkladze must get used to people trying to rattle him." It is open to question whether anyone can 'get used' to sustained physical abuse and it was perhaps more damning of the British game that opposing sides would stop at nothing to snuff out the stem of creativity threatening them. It's a man's game, true enough, but there are limits the body can endure and few players go into each game to be continually clattered. Fast forward a decade and maybe Kinkladze would have received better protection from the referees who are constantly under the media scrutiny in today's high-tech game full of cameras that seem to miss little. Anybody who witnessed some of the tackles going in on Kinky would be forced to admit that if the same treatment was given to Thierry Henry week in, week out, there would be an outcry. Arsene Wenger or Alex Ferguson would certainly ensure the whole world knew about the treatment their star player was receiving and maybe therein lies the crux of the matter. No City manager ever spoke up on his behalf – at least not loudly enough – so everyone thought everything was running at acceptable levels.

One Manchester derby was followed by another – the 'real' Manchester derby and a game crucial to both sides for vastly different reasons. United were chipping away at Newcastle's lead in the race for the Premiership crown while the Blues, with some tricky games to come, now realised the fight for survival was reaching the critical stage.

Mikhail Kavlashvili made his debut at the expense of an unhappy Uwe Rosler but even though he scored with a smart finish in the first half, City went down 3-2 and now had just four games to save themselves. Four became three as the Blues appeared on live television just two days later and looking jaded from their exertions against United the last the thing they needed was the physical challenge of Wimbledon at Selhurst Park. It was no surprise that they were out-muscled by 3-0 by the Dons. Prior to the next match, Francis Lee vowed to keep Kinky at Maine Road, even if the unthinkable happened and the club went down. "Georgi is going nowhere," he said defiantly. "We are looking to build a team around Gio, not to sell him. I'm looking for him to stay well into the next century and I can tell our supporters here and now that if this club ever slipped into a position where we had to sell Kinkladze then I would pack in the chairman's job."

Those were words Lee would be true to in the coming years. The team, no loner masters of their own destiny, found enough resolve to win their next two fixtures 1-0 against Sheffield Wednesday and Aston

Villa respectively. With one game to go, a win would ensure survival, but only if Southampton or Coventry City (on the same points but with better goal differences) failed to win.

With Liverpool - who included future City players Steve McManaman, David James and Robbie Fowler in the side - already guaranteed third spot whether they won or lost, this seemed like a game that City could win if they were on top of their game. But wins over the Merseyside Reds were rarer than rocking horse droppings and by half time, the Blues trailed 2-0 thanks to some slack defending. City looked as good as down. Kinkladze was determined to do everything he personally could to haul the Blues back from the brink and his endeavour and trickery won a penalty not long after the break. With the clock ticking, Kit Symons equalised with still 12 minutes to play – Maine Road roared the team on but despite their best efforts, they couldn't find the goal that would save them from the drop. Steve Lomas was ludicrously ordered to waste time by the bench who took a crowd rumour that Southampton were losing as gospel and moments later the final whistle went. All the wild rumours of what the other teams were doing was finally confirmed – Leeds and Southampton had both drawn their matches and City were relegated. Of all the pictures of the players leaving the pitch in tears, it was Kinkladze, wiping his reddened eyes with his jersey that sticks in the mind more than most. He - and perhaps a couple of other members of the team - didn't deserve relegation.

Now the club faced up to not only life in the Endsleigh League, but possibly life without Gio Kinkladze, whose wonderful ability was surely too grand for the nation's second tier of league football. His agent Jerome Anderson was seen having "an animated conversation" with Francis Lee shortly after the final whistle blew against Liverpool as invariably people put two and two together and wondered about where the Georgian would be playing his football the following season.

Not surprisingly, Gio won the Player of the Year by a landslide but most Blues were left dumbfounded that his March goal of the month against Southampton was only voted runner-up to Tony Yeboah's volley at Wimbledon. Great strike that Yeboah's was, it wasn't even half the goal it narrowly beat.

"It was a wonderful goal and brilliantly done and was the mark of a true star player," said Franny Lee. "It was an unbelievable goal and the amount of times he went close to scoring individual efforts very close to that was numerous." But as the nets were taken down for the summer at Maine Road and the supporters began thinking of games at Roots Hall and Blundell Park, Lee had things on his mind other than great goals. He had to sell the First Division, warts and all, to Georgi Kinkladze, now regarded by the fans as perhaps one of the best players to ever wear the sky blue of Manchester City. The fans braced themselves for more bad news, especially when Kinky's hero Diego Maradona was quoted in several tabloids as advising him not only to quit City, but England as well. Maradona said that Georgi should move to Italy and that he was made for Italian football. "He must move to Italy if he is to become a truly great footballer," said Maradona. "Playing in the English First Division could damage his career. Great players often pay a heavy price for their gift from God. I hope Kinkladze doesn't suffer too much if he stays in England. Italy is the one place where talent like his can truly reach the heights. My advice to him is: Go now." How the ears at Milan and Juventus must have pricked up... but would Georgi's?

Chapter 7
STAYING PUT

"The new contract is the most lucrative in the history of our club."

- Francis Lee

In the words of one of The Clash's more commercially successful tracks, the question Gio Kinkladze must have been asking himself as the Blues' fans dusted off road maps to Grimsby, Port Vale and Southend was 'Should I stay or should I go?' The argument for him to leave was overwhelming – how could a player who lit the Premiership up so many times in his first year waste his talents at Roots Hall, Blundell Park and half a dozen other charming – but tin-pot – lower league stadia?

This was a young man, still just 22, with the world as his feet, fit to grace the Bernabeu, Nou Camp or San Siro Stadium. It was unfair to even ask him to stay on when his career was clearly destined for bigger and better stages. It's probably true that he'd never find a set of supporters who idolised him like the City fans did but if he wanted to be the best and follow in his hero Diego Maradona's footsteps, he had to quit the Blues and maybe head for Italy. Yet Franny Lee felt certain he could convince him to stay and help the club Gio still clearly loved back to the Premiership. On the other side of the coin, one season out of the limelight wasn't the end of the world and he'd still only be 23 by the end of the 1996/97 season.

It's probably fair to say that Lee had become something of a surrogate father to Georgi having taken him under his wing since his move to Maine Road. He'd treated him like a son and spoke to him as a father would, telling him to wear bigger jumpers when it was cold, put a vest on in the winter and other parental touches. Lee knew Georgi was a lad who needed to feel he was part of a family and if he could help settle him, it would be the best thing for the player and the club.

"It wasn't a case of forming a bond with him," reasoned Lee. "We knew we had a lad who was an exceptional talent and we wanted him to stay. Everyone had to work at forming a bond with him. We got an interpreter to teach him English but after a few days, he got rid of her because she was Russian! The same thing happened with Uwe Rosler and we had to work hard to teach him the language and eventually we worked things out."

And Gio wouldn't forget that City had moved heaven and earth to get his mother over and even signed one of his pals on his recommendation. Being Georgian, he was a loyal and proud man and if Francis Lee asked him to stay, he was not going to let him or the supporters who worshipped him down. So a new contract was drawn up and Gio put pen to paper on a deal designed to keep him at the club until 1999. But perhaps there was more to it than feeling he owed Manchester City a favour. He'd found a home where he could be himself, play his way and was adored by the supporters. It was a lot to give up, whatever situation the club had found itself in.

"He wanted to stay because he loved the place," said Lee. "But he had an agent - or adviser - who was also his interpreter and he was wanted him to move on and was always leaking stories to the paper about him wanting to move on, but it wasn't true – he wanted to stay and he'd still be at City to this day if things had worked out differently. He needed good players to play alongside him and needed protection in midfield. He also needed good strong players who would stick their foot in because he was a free role player, a bit like Eric Cantona – he'd find his little space and then make things happen from there. But if he was man-to-man marked, as he was so often, all of sudden he couldn't do that as effectively.

"There were a lot of clubs interested and that wanted him but you had to be interested in that type of player – a playmaker with exceptional skill – to really want him. A lot of managers don't like players like that but there were two or three clubs who said if we were interested in selling him to let them know. We said, okay, fine, but we didn't want to sell him. We thought we could build a team around him and he could take us back to the Premiership and from there go on to bigger and better things."

The Press, who had been full of stories of who was likely to win the race to sign the Georgian were rocked by the news he'd agreed to stay at Maine Road but the City fans were understandably elated. It was the lift the club needed ahead of what was going to be a crucial and very tough season. City would be everyone's cup final, but with Gio on board, they would surely sail back into the Premiership. First, though, it was a much-awaited return to his native Georgia to spend quality time with friends and family and have time to reflect on the impact he'd made in his first full season abroad.

This time around, Gio could look forward to a proper pre-season training programme and could also build his fitness up during the pre-season friendlies, something he didn't have the luxury of the previous year. With no civil war to worry about at Dinamo and no uncertainty about which foreign club he would be loaned out to next, he was at last feeling settled. Within the last 18 months he'd been at Dinamo, Atletico

Madrid, Real Madrid, Saarbrucken and Boca Juniors and travelled around the world in search of a permanent home. Now he had one and he returned from Tbilisi refreshed and ready for the challenge of helping his club back into the top flight at the first time of asking.

There had been no managerial change at Maine Road with Ball entrusted with tasking of getting the club out of the hole many people thought he'd got them in. City left for Ireland in July and with Niall Quinn looking in sparkling form, they brushed aside Athlone Town and Cork City, 3-1 in each game. Gio, who seemed to be carrying a few extra pounds (probably too much home cooked treats by relatives keen to remind him what he was missing) and was less than impressive in either game, his mind no doubt still several thousand miles away in Tbilisi.

The Blues then jetted out to China to play three games – but the ill-fated tour saw just one game – against Tianjin – take place and the other two matches called off due to torrential rain, flash floods and monsoons reducing parts of the country to a disaster area. Only City could pick that particular time to visit!

Photographer Kevin Cummins, whose pictures of The Smiths and Joy Division in their pomp established him as one of the leaders in his field, had flown out to support the team with several friends and recalled a couple of occasions he met Gio – one which was quite unforgettable. "It was quite obvious the players didn't want to be there," he said. "I recall the only game that actually went ahead against Tianjin – the ground was an absolute shed and I went to the toilet before the game to be greeted with what amounted to about one hundred years of piss and shit that had never been properly cleaned. Who should walk in but Georgi Kinkladze – he took one look around and then threw up!

"Later, we were in this hotel bar – all the fans who'd travelled over and the team were staying at the same place – and Alan Ball invited us over to his table and told us that if we were prepared to travel to China to support the team, the least he could do was buy our beer. There was ten or so of us in our group and he wouldn't let us buy another drink. He even got on the Karaoke and when Uwe Rosler walked in he said 'I'd like to dedicate this song to Uwe' before singing 'And I Love You So'! Uwe slammed down his beer, gave Ball the one-fingered salute and stormed out. Gio came into the bar after that and just sat chatting with us all and buying everyone drinks. He was just a really nice guy."

The Blues returned home none-the-wiser from their Chinese adventure and travelled to the East Coast for their next warm-up game. Many of the fans that made the journey to Scarborough to watch City scramble a 2-2 draw seemed concerned about the lack of Kinky's pre-season form. It would be understandable if he were homesick but was it also possible that friends and former teammates had filled his head with thoughts of where they believed he should be playing? It's hard to believe nobody expressed concern or opinions about him playing football in the English First Division. City completed their tour in Devon with a win at Exeter and defeat at Plymouth – Gio was substituted in both games - but the general feeling was the Blues would get it right for the big kick off... optimism is a wonderful thing in the wrong hands.

On August 14, City held their first ever Open Day at Maine Road and with thousands in attendance, the afternoon reached fever pitch with the appearance of Georgi Kinkladze. He was mobbed as soon as he walked onto the pitch by more than 1,000 young autograph hunters who swarmed across the pitch to meet their idol up close. City's security guards had to escort him to the safety of the dressing rooms while things calmed down. If he had needed reminding of his status amongst the City support, he had seen it uo close in that mass stampede.

Two days later, the Blues kicked off the new English season by taking on Ipswich Town in a live televised Friday night game at Maine Road. If Gio had looked rusty for the friendlies he was back to his usual self for the opening game of the campaign and it was his cross that allowed Steve Lomas to head the only goal of the game and give the team the start they desperately needed. On paper, City had a squad that should have comfortably been promoted, but few could have predicted the rocky months ahead for the club or the bruising encounters ahead for Kinky and his army of 'markers'.

"The hackers were definitely after him and I think he found that hard to deal with, especially with the drop down from the Premiership," said Nick Summerbee. "There wasn't much we could do as a team to protect him but we all thought we'd come straight back up and perhaps weren't prepared for battling in 46 matches. Because we were Manchester City, they tried that much harder to beat us and with Georgi being the star man, they just tried to cancel him out anyway they could. It was hard for him.

"In the Premiership there was all the glitz and glamour that went with it and the adrenaline was pumping each week. But sometimes in the First Division, it felt different and you might not know the opponents you are playing against – if it's Manchester United or Liverpool every week, you are up for it all the time but despite there being 30,000 people in the stadium, some of the teams we were playing made it hard to feel that way. Georgi was playing against defenders he could roast all day but there were two or three players kicking lumps out of him and it became quite difficult for him.

"I think Alan Ball knew how to play him best. He had a real go with him. Georgi needed a bit of an arm around him to show him he was needed and Ball definitely did that."

Who could have predicted that, just two games later, Alan Ball would quit his position as manager of Manchester City as his position became untenable. A gutless defeat at Bolton and another flat display and loss at Stoke, where both sets of fans chanted for Ball's resignation, was enough for the former England World Cup winner to leave what been a largely unhappy period of his (and the City fans') life behind him. The club was in turmoil with only three games gone and their pre-season favourites tag already looked generous in the extreme.

Speculation in the Press intensified over Gio's future and Celtic's name was linked with a £10million 'swoop' on more than one occasion, causing chairman Lee to again respond angrily, claiming the stories to be "nonsense." But, of course, this story and a dozen others would not go away.

George Graham seemed to be the man City wanted to replace Ball but that would have surely spelled the end for Kinkladze – Graham was old school and didn't really 'do' flair players and would have almost certainly considered him a luxury, especially at First Division level. So the Blues ran out against Charlton without a boss and for most of the game, that was abundantly clear. The visitors comfortably led 1-0 until the 83rd minute when a foul on Ball's last signing as manager - Paul Dickov - resulted in a penalty. Rosler tucked the spot-kick away and then Gerry Creaney surprised everyone with a super free kick four minutes later, to win the game. Despite the result, it had been an appalling game and the sooner City installed a new manager, the better.

Defeat at home to Barnsley and victory at Port Vale, where Kinky had his best game of the season so far, but was subjected to yet more X-certificate 'tackles'. On a more encouraging note, it seemed that if Gio did come in for any special attention, it always seemed to infuriate him and he responded by making the offender look a complete mug. This was an admirable side to his game considering some of the punishment dished out in his direction was at least double that of his first season, plus he invariably had a minimum of two markers each game. Gio also celebrated a new boot deal with Diadora around that time, with *The Mirror* claiming it could net the City star up to £600,000 over three years, which was perhaps slightly exaggerated. Meanwhile, another loss at Crystal Palace, where the Eagles' manager Dave Bassett was believed to be taking his last game in charge before becoming City's new boss (he didn't) was followed by arguably one of the worst performances and results of City's modern era. A 4-1 hammering by Third Division Lincoln City in the Coca-Cola Cup demonstrated the Blues' dire need to get a new man to save what was already a desperate looking season. Gio's absence from this debacle, probably wise seeing the Imps' reputation for physical and often bruising encounters, also started a media whisper campaign that he'd been left out so as not to be cup-tied – but were the Blues really planning to sell their prized asset? Several tabloids suggested Arsenal and Liverpool were planning £5million (relegation had clearly reduced his stock) moves in the near future. Caretaker boss Asa Hartford told reporters Gio was missing due a hamstring injury – no more, no less - but why let the truth spoil a good story?

Kinky played in the next game and also took over the mantle of penalty taker from Uwe Rosler scoring the only goal in the last minute against Birmingham City. He was also in the return Coca-Cola Cup clash with Lincoln City, which, incredibly, ended with another defeat and a 1-5 aggregate loss overall – one of the worst results in City's proud history and certainly on a par with the FA Cup 3rd round loss at Halifax Town 16 years earlier. Another defeat at Sheffield United was followed by yet another man-of-the match performance by Gio in a 2-2 draw at QPR. He bagged another penalty but was imperious all evening, tormenting the home defence to the point of cruelty but as so often, his hard work met with little reward. But the topsy-turvy Blues continued to outwit the fixed odds coupons consistently, first losing at Reading, then beating Norwich. The latter game saw Steve Coppell take a bow in front of the Kippax after agreeing, at last, to become the new City boss and thus ending the ten-game period without a manager. The only way was up, so everyone thought.

Chapter 8
GEORGIA ON HIS MIND

Georgi's boyhood hero was Grigol Tsaava, one of the leading lights of the 1980s Dinamo team and he watched from the terraces of the Boris Paichadze Stadium as the skilful Tbilisi star weaved his magic. It's believed that Kinky based his precocious talent on Tsaava's skills and at one point, he realised his dream when Tsaava, who had been away fighting the civil war for two years, returning a hero to Tbilisi to play football again. But so affected by the conflict was the player that his comeback lasted just two games.

Tsaava had witnessed death and destruction at close hand and mentally was not prepared to play football again and, bearing jagged psychological scars, he played just 180 minutes before retiring. Georgi played in the same side but it was a bitter and moving experience for the young midfielder and one that he has never forgotten.

Determined to do something positive for Georgian football, which was littered with many such stories of despair and anguish, Georgi, along with his father Robizon, helped raise Lokomotovi from the ashes of extinction, 15 years after they had last played league football. Georgi was putting something back into the Georgian game and resurrecting one of the great teams from the past made him one of the players in the world who also owned a club.

"Many of the players from Georgia who have gone abroad have not helped people back home like Gio did," said Robizon. "But these are Gio's friends that he grew up with, and some are former team-mates, so he wanted to help them."

So in June, 1996 Lokomotovi were re-born thanks to the money Georgi Kinkladze was sending home. It was a terrific gesture from a man who never forgot what others gave to help give his homeland its independence. Thanks to his move to City, he was able to send around £5,000 per month – about half of the club's monthly outgoings – with the average monthly wage in Georgia around £15 at the time. Gio also sent kits, balls and other equipment to help the club get on its feet.

Crumbling tower blocks, laced with washing lines, surrounded the Lokomotovi ground and the second floor of the team offices was home to 26 families, refugees from the war. Tbilisi itself escaped much of the conflicts but was still suffering battles on its streets from organised crime gangs who have been responsible for a number of deaths of players, officials and notaries over the years. In 1995, when Georgi left Tbilisi, it was impossible for any Western businessmen to travel on the streets without an armed guard. Shoot-outs between rival gangs were a regular occurrence and it's no wonder Merab Jordania was eager to get the young Tbilisi talent shipped overseas and to relative safety.

In fact, the Georgian football team became the epitome of national pride following the break-up of the tyrannical Soviet regime and as the country slowly recovered from years of war and organised crime, the country's footballers became heroic figures; icons rising from the rubble. None more so than the most exciting young talent to ever come from Georgia, Gio Kinkladze.

"A lot of people went to war without knowing how to use a gun," recalled Georgi. "Hardships on the field are nothing by comparison."

Chapter 9

MANAGING TO GET BY

"My thinking was that you can get anyone to run back and fill the right holes but you can't get people to do what Gio could do."

– **Steve Coppell**

That England had drawn Georgia in their World Cup qualifying group left many City fans with something of a quandary. What if one of the England players clattered into Kinkladze? Where would the loyalty lie? What if he scored one of his magical goals? Did they cheer or watch impassively? It was a case of 'wait and see' but it at least allowed Georgi the chance to show his talents were undiminished on a world stage rather than just amidst the First Division cloggers.

The first of the two games between the countries took place in Tbilisi, allowing Gio to return home again, this time on 'official business', to represent his homeland. He'd been part of the squad that had just missed out on the European Championships in 1996 and now Georgia prepared for perhaps the biggest game of its short life as an independent country. Gio took time out to visit a local orphanage to visit children affected by the war and high crime rate and he promised them to do his best to help beat the country where he earned his living. Needless to say, England had signalled him out as their major threat.

"I owe it to my country to produce my best form on Saturday," he said prior to the game. "I have played against most of the England side with the exception of Paul Ince and Paul Gascoigne and I know what type of threat they pose. But we have many players who are comfortable on the ball and believe that if England try to match us at passing, they could be destroyed."

In the event, England won 2-0, despite the best efforts of the Georgians and Kinky was well marked throughout the game but afterwards, England boss Glenn Hoddle admitted he admired the Manchester City star. "It was a good all-round display with some fine individual performances," said Hoddle. "We gave the Georgians a lot of respect. It's not an easy place to come and win but we probably deserved it. Georgi Kinkladze is a superb footballer, but we stopped him playing today. We got the early goal and that gave us a good lift and confidence."

Back in Manchester, Gio was flying into the eye of the storm – after just one month in charge, Steve Coppell, who'd made such a favourable impression on the player during his short stay, had resigned because he felt the job was making him ill. His assistant Phil Neal was placed in charge on a temporary basis as the Blues concentrated on the clash with Oxford United. What Gio must have been thinking at this point isn't hard to guess and if his thoughts were beginning to drift away from playing for City, who could have blamed him? Playing for his country in front of more than 70,000 fans against England one minute, then being beaten by a poor Oxford United amidst a team that had no direction, little quality and a succession of managers who hadn't a clue what to do for the best, the next.

Coppell, who had lasted just 30 days in the hot seat at Maine Road recalls what it was like managing a talent such as Gio's and admits he wasn't aware at the time that Gio held him in such high esteem.

"In my short time at City I soon found that I agreed with Francis Lee's assessment of Georgi," said Coppell whose Reading side was challenging strongly for promotion at the time. "I knew I had a special talent in the team but the problem I had was working out how best to use him. I didn't want to make him a 'hod carrier' in the team and decided to just give him the freedom to express himself and get other people to do the donkeywork, as it were.

"I wanted to give him as free a role as possible and I think he responded to that whilst other people thought – I think - that wasn't perhaps the right thing to do because in English football the perception is everybody has to chase back and do this and do that. My thinking was that you can get anyone to run back and fill the right holes but you can't get people to do what Gio could do, so I was just desperate to get him to do what he did best and that was by giving him as little defensive responsibility as possible.

"People would say that I couldn't do that and that he should be working harder and tracking back more but I said they should look at things the other way. The responsibility I gave him was more in many ways because he had to create things and make goal for other people and score himself. If he wasn't creating, he wasn't producing. In that City side at the time, there was nobody who could do what he could do. Admittedly, he could have one good game, one average game and maybe two bad games and get away with it, but I was trying to put the burden of responsibility back on his shoulders.

"I told him it wasn't about having one good game in four and that he didn't have to do all the donkeywork, but in turn he had to produce with creation and unfortunately that's something a lot of English people can't understand because it's a working class game and everyone's supposed to muck in together. But with Georgi, I felt it was different.

"His English wasn't that good when I was there and he didn't say that much – Nicky Summerbee seemed to be his interpreter when the need arose. They used to go out together socially and I asked Nicky, 'How does he get on with the birds?' and Nicky said that Gio had a great chat-up line. I asked him what it was and he said that Gio would say 'I have got big house would you like to come see?'

"So although I didn't really know him too well, I always thought the language barrier held him back from interacting too much with the other lads but he was always very amenable and seemed popular. There was no special privileges for him at training but you do obviously have to treat people differently - but if he'd been late or whatever, I'd have treated him the same as anyone else."

Kinkladze had stated that he was upset about Coppell's shock departure and said he'd admired his management style and felt he would have got the very best out of his game. Coppell admits he was unaware of this tribute to his style of coaching.

"I hate to say it - and it's my loss more than anyone else's - but I did hibernate a bit after quitting City," Coppell confessed. "If Georgi did say those things about me, that's great, but I did miss a great opportunity at City and I would have certainly enjoyed working with him. It's a conundrum with him because I'm sure he's looking back at his whole career so far thinking it's not anything like it should have been and it would have been a hell of a test for any manager to get the very best out of him and fit him into the framework of the team."

The Press, never behind the door at exploiting such situations were determined to help Kinky on his way and tracked down his European representative, German Wolfgang Voege, who it was claimed said: "If we had a good offer for Georgi, he would go tomorrow. He is not happy at all with things at Manchester City. There is interest, not only from France, Italy, Germany but also a number of English clubs."

Francis Lee reacted with anger saying there had been no approaches and felt it was all part of a plan to unsettle the player.

"He is as good as gold and just wants leaving alone," fumed Lee. "When he sees reports linking him with other clubs, he naturally wants to know if there is anything going on. There isn't. He is under contract until 1999." Lee went on to reveal there was no get-out clause in Kinky's contract allowing him to leave for not winning promotion or for any other reason. His London-based agent Jerome Anderson confirmed his client remained a Manchester City player unless the club decided otherwise. But Anderson apart, sometimes the outside interference of some 'advisors' was open to question and it appeared Gio had a succession of people attempting to 'represent' him for reasons best know to themselves.

The tabloid mischief continued unabated until Gio, who'd by this time had his fill of the English media, took the unusual step of issuing a statement through his London agent stating he had no wish to leave the club and that he fully supported the chairman and that's how things would stay until he informed them otherwise. City, meanwhile, continued to stumble down the table under the largely ineffectual leadership of Phil Neal, who to be fair, was given a pretty thankless task. Defeats at Portsmouth and miserable home performances against Tranmere (1-2) and Huddersfield Town (0-0) failed to lighten the heavy black clouds gathering over Maine Road once more.

But at least the Blues had a player who, on his day, could destroy the opposition virtually on his own and Kinky, now wearing his favourite No.10 shirt, gave just about the perfect midfield display as City beat West Brom 3-2, adding two more goals to take his season's tally to six. He added two more in the next three games, with his masterful chip at Oldham Athletic - where he was again subjected to something amounting to assault at the hands of the Latics players – a thing of beauty. The opening of the month-long transfer window had not brought in any bids, despite the sustained media speculation. Possible suitors such as Barcelona, Real Betis, Parma and Inter Milan were all reported to be moving in on the player with the predicted auction set to reach £10million. Gut-wrenching defeats to Port Vale and Barnsley left City fourth from bottom of the table and Phil Neal, either off his own bat or after a word in his ear, announced his resignation.

Next please!

Frank Clark was next into the Maine Road hot-seat which was now allegedly leaving griddle marks on the behind of anybody who dared sit in it - and so came the numerous reports of what the new man planned to do with Gio: where to play or not to play him/when he would sell him/ if he would sell him, etc (delete as applicable). Then the News of the World, hardly the soccer bible when it came to events at Maine Road, revealed their 'world exclusive'. As the price on Gio's head fluctuated from day to day, apparently Clark was sizing up a swap deal with Newcastle United's Lee Clark plus £2.5million. As ever, the story was denied in the Manchester Evening News the next day with Clark not about to commit the equivalent of soccer suicide by selling the fans' hero for his first act as manager.

A cold snap prevented Clark's managerial debut until January 11, 1997 when City drew 1-1 with Crystal Palace. It was also the first time Clark saw the equivalent of a 'soccer nasty' in the flesh as he witnessed first hand the type of challenges Kinkladze was being subjected to during 90 minutes of action. In fact, Robert Hopkin (the assigned hatchet man of that particular day) made a challenge that resulted with the Kinky being stretchered off after lying prostrate for several minutes. He managed to hobble down the tunnel, but it didn't look good. For Palace it was a case of job done. But Clark, never really associated with the attractive cavalier approach that City fans loved was clearly having problems working out Gio's place in the increasingly mixed up puzzle that was the City team.

"Frank Clark was in charge at that time and after about three months at the club, he asked me what Gio's best position was!" revealed Francis Lee. "I thought, bloody hell, you're supposed to be the manager! He had a coach there, Richard Money and he was supposed to be a good coach and they didn't know what Gio's best position was."

How much more punishment and behind-the-scenes torment was Kinkladze prepared to put up with? Things were going from bad to worse and, for the first time in his career, the forward momentum of his career had stalled and was threatening to go into reverse.

Chapter 10
ONE MORE FOR THE ROAD?

'How can I leave this place when there are so many people who love me so much?'

– Georgi Kinkladze

With four days to go before the end of another deflating season at Maine Road, Georgi Kinkladze prepared with the rest of the Georgian squad to face England at Wembley. As kid, he had kicked a ball around the back streets of Tbilisi, dreaming of playing at the home of world football, threading balls through to Kenny Dalglish or Ian Rush for Liverpool. Now he was about to play for his country against the English on a stage worthy of his skills. And he wouldn't disappoint, showing some magical touches and being a thorn in England's side until he limped off on 60 minutes with a recurrence of a groin injury. The applause as he departed the pitch could have been for an England player; such was the appreciation from the Wembley crowd who clearly held him in high esteem. England won by the same score they had in Tbilisi – 2-0 - but, worryingly for City fans, Kinky was now also ruled out of the final league game of the season at home to Reading and many wondered if his appearance at Ipswich the previous week might even have been his last in City's colours.

Franny Lee had insisted Gio would be playing for City for the 1997/98 season and claimed it was "odds on" that he would commit to at least one more season, with a re-tailored deal to suit his demands. "There's only been one enquiry for Gio," said Lee at the time. "I told them to go away and not bother me again and they did." But for the football world in general, it was inconceivable that Kinkladze would waste another year playing Endsleigh League football. The City fans, too, knew their hero must be thinking of pastures new after one of the most traumatic seasons in the club's history, but they were determined to not let him go without a fight. With one game left of the 1996/97 season, the City supporters' clubs rallied together to think up ways of convincing Kinkladze to stay. He may not have been playing against Reading but he would hpefully be taking part in any end of season lap of honour.

So it was that Georgi Kinkladze Day was born

The result would send shivers down the spines of those who witnessed the events of May 3, 1997. For many of the Blues' followers, watching Gio strut his stuff at any level – international, club or even on the training ground at Platt Lane, was the one silver lining to a black storm cloud that seemed to have become rather attached to Manchester City. Here was a precocious talent that came along perhaps once in blue moon, so to speak, and the pleasure he gave his army of admirers almost made up for the more often than not below average fayre on offer week in, week out. A feint, swivel of the hips, nutmeg or delicately chipped pass would lift the crowd, even if they were trailing 1-0 at home to the likes of Lincoln City. Gio made them all forget how bad things were and without him, the club's future looked bleak.

Of course he had quiet games and sometimes the best part of 90 minutes might pass him by. But that could apply to many players, especially some of the journeymen playing for the Blues around that time, and the fact remained, a Kinkladze off day was still a reasonable performance for most. Fans organised petitions, messages and banners written in Georgian, along with flags and flashing scoreboard messages to be displayed during the game. If he had even the merest doubt as to how the fans still felt about him, this would allay them once and for all. Whatever happened that afternoon against Reading, the supporters knew it had to be special. Particularly with Liverpool, Barcelona and Inter Milan believed to be closing in for the kill, just waiting for the nod of approval from the City chairman to begin negotiations to take him away from Maine Road.

Of course, Franny Lee was close to the player and his relationship to the fans and ties to Manchester was strong. Yet despite what the chairman claimed, many believed he had no option but to move on. Surely he had to get his career back on track? As Gio watched from the Main Stand, his teammates did their best to convince him to move on, going 2-0 down to Reading after just 33 minutes. The chanting for Kinkladze went on throughout the game and the flags waved and banners were displayed, all proclaiming that he should stay at Maine Road, his spiritual home. One repetitive song in particular: "He's got to stay, he's got to stay, he's got to, Kinky's got to stay," was sang throughout the 90 minutes and it seemed to inspire the rest of the team as they fought back to win a thrilling game 3-2. The final whistle went, the players trooped down the tunnel and an entire crowd waited to see what would happen next.

There were a few minutes before the team re-emerged for the planned lap of honour, though there had been precious little honour in the past nine months. Every member of the squad walked back out, with Kinkladze, in a light brown suit, at the back. As the team went around the ground, the club's matchday announcer, Vince Miller, who had been with the club since 1966, took hold of Gio's arm and led him out into the middle of the pitch where he received rapturous applause and cheers from all four sides of the ground. He looked a little uncomfortable with the special attention and at being separated from his teammates but he applauded back at his adoring public as they sang and waved to him.

Miller, who stayed with Kinkladze until he eventually left the pitch a good ten minutes later, recalled how things looked from his own unique viewpoint, almost seeing the adulation through Gio's eyes.

"When I arrived at the ground that day, Francis Lee asked me to go and see him," Miller revealed. "He told me Gio wasn't going to play due to an injury but he'd come out at the end of the game and I was to take him to the centre circle, let him wave to the fans and that was it.

"The game ended and the players left the pitch and then re-emerged shortly after. Gio came out behind them as they began walking around the perimeter of the pitch and I took him aside and began to lead him out to the centre circle, as I'd been asked to. Uwe Rosler took exception to this and came over to me to make his feelings known and we exchanged a few heated words. He thought it wasn't right but I did was I was asked and led Gio out to the middle of Maine Road, which I believe is what the fans would have wanted anyway.

"Gio's English wasn't very good but he said to me it was a very sad day for him. The fans had Georgian flags everywhere and messages written in his language. He looked moved by what he was seeing but didn't want to talk too much about it. He was very relaxed, having said that. The fans had given him an amazing ovation. I felt justified in taking him aside and after all, I was just doing what Francis asked. I'm quite sure Gio was planning to leave before that day."

Rosler's anger wasn't aimed at his teammate but the frustration at being one of the 'other ten' probably boiled over that afternoon. It must have been hard for the rest of the team to be so far in the shadows but the majority seemed to understand it better than they are perhaps ever given credit for.

"It was a bit odd him being led out like that, but we all saw it the way Georgi did – it was hard for him and we all understood that," said Nick Summerbee who was one of the 'other ten' that day. "If he was a bit big time in the dressing room for all the adulation he was receiving, he might have got a bit of friction for it, but he wasn't. Everyone knew what he was all about and understood why the fans loved him and we just got on with it, really."

He appeared looked visibly moved as he passed the Kippax and some took that to be as good as a farewell. He completed his walk around with a final wave and then went back down the tunnel. The City fans filed out into the warm summer sunshine and kept their fingers crossed. They'd done their bit, now they had to let the chairman get on with the business end of things. The general consensus was still the same – Gio was leaving City but if that was the case, it was at least nice that the Blues' support had had the opportunity to say 'thanks' for two magnificent years.

Whatever Georgi's thoughts were as he made his way home later that day are known only to him but chances are he was being torn apart mentally and emotionally. The burning desire to play at the top level was being weighed up against loyalty to the fans who had shown their appreciation in unprecedented ways with an outpouring of affection not seen since Colin Bell made an emotional comeback on Boxing Day, 1977. In fact the mention of Bell's name around this time was likely to start animated conversations, often between young and old as to which was City's greatest ever player. The likes of Bert Trautmann, Eric Brook, Peter Doherty and Billy Meredith would be mentioned but inevitably, the Bell v Kinkladze argument would eventually take centre stage. Of course, in terms of achievement, Bell would have to take the mantle but for skill and pure individual and technical ability, none could come close to Kinkladze, who, it has to be said, was playing in a team that struggled for two seasons with countless managers coming and going. Bell was in a team of winners with the best management team the club has ever had. Talent always shines through but the one thing Gio never played in was a truly exceptional team and that would remains a constant factor throughout his career.

"To understand Georgi, you need to understand certain things about the Georgian mentality. We are very warm people, and also very loyal," said Koba Bekeria, Gio's brother-in-law. "When the Manchester City fans welcomed Georgi into their hearts that meant a great deal to him.

"There was a time when Barcelona, Arsenal, and Liverpool all wanted him... but he resisted because of the support of the City fans. He could have left when City got relegated – he stayed because of the fans. I remember how moved he was when he saw fans coming to his house in Wilmslow with Georgian flags and banners with the words: Don't go Gio. That made a big impression on him."

Four days after the completion of the season, the gifted Georgian was crowned Player of the Year for the second successive time. His close pal, Nicky Summerbee, was runner-up. Again, Gio was mobbed by anxious fans at the City Social Club and in response to one of the many supporters' questions about whether he would remain a Blue for another year he said, "Yes, maybe." Franny Lee was again working feverishly to keep the player but he faced a mammoth task to convince him that a second year of First Division football was better than pursuing a glamorous career on the continent or elsewhere in Britain.

His sister Marina reveals a fascinating insight to the inner struggles Gio was wrestling with: "One fan presented him with an album of cuttings from the whole of his career up to that point. You can't imagine how many people came to his house with gifts and suchlike. He said at the time: 'How can I leave this place when there are so many people who love me so much?'"

The Georgian FA were adding extra pressure by claiming, not unfairly, they preferred their international stars to be playing top level football wherever they earned their wages. Whatever deal Lee could offer, it would have to be weighed off by a hefty financial package and a specially tailored (and effectively a one-year plan) to tempt the player, with various clauses to satisfy his now numerous representatives. It seemed Gio had acquired agents based all over the world and with the big bucks on the table, they all wanted a slice and how helpful some of them actually were for the player and City is not hard to guess.

The Manchester Evening News claimed Kinky had demanded £1million to stay one more year, plus a 20 per cent cut of any transfer fee the Blues received if they decided to sell in that period. Locked in talks at Lee's house, the chairman had used his not inconsiderable charm, business acumen and relationship with Gio to convince him it was worth one more try. Gio is no fool and aside from the money, he knew in leaving City he would be giving up the type of relationship with the fans the only a select few enjoyed throughout the world. Diego Maradona at Napoli, Eric Cantona at Manchester United and Gabriel Batistuta at

Roma are three that spring to mind but they are the exception rather than the rule. In fact, the fans were still taking every opportunity to let Gio know what he meant to them and one night out with Nick Summerbee and Fitzroy Simpson, one man got down on one knee and, with tears in his eyes, begged him to stay – what the poor besotted chap couldn't have known was that Gio had already made his mind up what he was going to do.

GEORGIAN BROTHERS: Gio flanked by Shota Averladze (left) and Khakbar Tshkadadze (right)

RELEGATED: A tearful Gio is helped by Eike Immel and a steward after City's 1996 relegation

STATING PUT: City fans launch a charm offensive to convince Gio to stay one more season after failing to win promotion back to the top flight at the first attempt.

WALK THIS WAY: Gio walks around the pitch after the final match of the 1996/97 season with announcer Vince Hill.

WRECK: The mangled remains of Gio's Ferrari which he was lucky to walk away from.

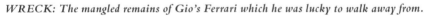

END OF AN ERA: Gio waves goodbye after coming on as a sub in the 5-2 win at Stoke in 1998 - but it wasn't enough to prevent a second relegation in three seasons and would be Gio's last game for City.

SAINT GIO: On his way to scoring an incredible solo goal against Southampton in 1996.

GOING DUTCH: Gio signs for Ajax in 1998

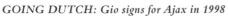

WING AND A PRAYER: Ajax employed Gio as a winger rather than an attacking central midfielder.

NOT HAPPY: The move to Ajax was not a good one for Gio who was unhappy in Amsterdam.

ANGUISH: Not much went right with the Dutch giants

BENCH DUTY: Kinky watches on from the sidelines during an Ajax match.

BACK IN ENGLAND: Georgi found a new lease of life with Derby County.

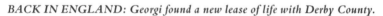

PHOTO-SHOOT: With the Rams...

WELCOME HOME: Georgi takes on Alfie Haaland in a clash with City at Maine Road. He received a hero's welcome

BOLTON BOY: A short spell with the Trotters for Gio.

Chapter 11

ONE TOO MANY?

"I asked for a lot of money but not out of greed. I just wanted to secure the future of my family and even my friends back home in Georgia who I want to help."

– Georgi Kinkladze

On May 17, 1997 Manchester City announced Georgi Kinkladze would be staying at Maine Road. It was news the football world could scarcely believe but it was manna from heaven for his legion of fans at the club. Francis Lee deserved full credit for convincing the 23 year-old to give it one more go and he was, quite rightly, proud of the deal. "Everyone at Maine Road is delighted that Gio has signed a new three-year contract and our supporters will be equally overjoyed," said Lee shortly after the story broke.

Outsiders reckoned that if staying the previous season had been a questionable decision, an extra season playing down amongst the dead men amounted to something close to career suicide. If City struggled again in the next 12 months, the impetus and reputation Gio had built up in his first year at the club would surely be in shreds but, thanks to fan-power and his relationship with the chairman, he'd shown amazing loyalty – a rare attribute in the modern game. To some it represented little more than the doting son who stays at home to care for a dependent relative and watches his own hopes and dreams fade as time moves on. To others it proved that not all top footballers were greedy, self-motivated publicity seekers, even if the remuneration package was not insubstantial.

Figures were bandied around in the media and some factions of the national press seemed to shift ominously away from Kinkladze, perhaps because he wasn't playing ball with their lofty stories that usually began with "Barcelona, Milan, Liverpool..." and so on. If he was going to prove their 'exclusives' continually wrong, he was going to have to pay the price. First off the mark was Phil Shirley in *The People* a day after the deal had been announced. Gio was quoted with lengthy dialogue that would have amazed his close friends who had only ever heard the shy young man speak a few sentences in English. Yet here, he was fluent and masterful of the language, pleading with City fans not to break his heart. He may, of course, have spoken through an interpreter though it seemed odd as he rarely if ever spoke to journalists.

"I am not greedy. It is not in my nature," Kinkladze was quoted as saying. "I asked for a lot of money but not out of greed. I just wanted to secure the future of my family and even my friends back home in Georgia who I want to help.

"I only asked for what I consider to be fair in comparison to what other internationals are earning. I do not earn a lot of money now compared with other top players in English football and it has cost me in terms of personal sacrifice to make a career in England."

The report also claimed Gio had been abused by some City fans that believed he was ripping off the Blues, adding that one man had told him "the fans were disgusted." Strange, seeing as the deal was only announced the afternoon before, with no firm financial details released. It's not inconceivable that all this could have happened, but considering what the City fans had done to convince him to stay, it seems a little at odds with all that had happened before. Could it possibly have been a supporter of a team not too far from City? Clubs crawled out of the woodwork from all over Europe to explain to their fans that Kinkladze's hefty wage demands had deterred them from signing him. Fiorentina, it was suggested, were quoted £3.5million in wage demands over two years and Turkish giants Galatasaray were another alleged to have been told that Gio wanted – this time - £1.5m over three years. Quite a fluctuation! One quote from the president of that club, Frank Suran, indicated "the player in question should sack the people who represent him" because he felt they were hampering his career. This wouldn't be the first time this had been said about some of the people claiming to have Georgi's best interests at heart, though it is perhaps not fair to tar all with the same brush.

The most reliable source of information at this time was Bryan Brett at the *Manchester Evening News*. In a story entitled 'Just fan-tastic', Kinky said of the fans: "I want to thank them for their support. I have always been happy here. Manchester is my home." No mention of abusive fans there, then. If a picture does, indeed, tell a thousand words, however, the photo that accompanied the piece, with Francis Lee and Bernard Halford sat either side of Gio as he signed the new deal, it was this particular image. The smile is a little subdued and his eyes almost burn through the lens. What exactly was he thinking? Perhaps he was genuinely happy but as he signed the new contract, he just looked a little distant. Perhaps the mental anguish of what had gone at City the previous season was finally taking its toll. Soon after, he flew home to Georgia to reflect on the new deal and enjoy the summer with his family as well as preparing for a couple of World Cup qualifiers for his country. He returned in time for pre-season training and again selected the squad No. 10 to accompany the new, laser blue home shirts. Unlike last season's largely disastrous warm-up matches, City remained unbeaten in all eight games and were again amongst the red-hot favourites to win promotion.

Meanwhile, Francis Lee revealed that the Blues had been close to signing Gio's childhood friend Shota Averladze from Ajax little more than a year earlier and had he joined, it may well have re-shaped the fortunes of the club dramatically.

"It was touch and go whether Shota Averladze came or not," said Lee. "Up until we were relegated he was coming but when we went down he decided not to sign and quite rightly so. So we signed Mikhail Kavlashvili instead, who did okay for us, but Frank Clark didn't like him and I thought he was a fair player. Clark signed players including a winger from Sunderland, Barry Conlon and a few other players who were also supposed to be better than Kavlashvili but in my opinion, none of them were as good. But it suited Clark to leave him out of the side because the lad couldn't speak much English so if someone needed to make way, it was Kav. He scored on his debut against United as well."

For Kinkladze, he had reached a crossroads point in his career. He was now being paid big bucks and he would be expected to earn them every time he played, even by the fans that idolised him. That this was another year in the First Division was barely palatable to everyone connected to the club but the thought of promotion kept things ticking along. A third consecutive campaign out of the top flight was even more unthinkable and everyone would be looking to Gio to inspire the Blues back to the Premiership where they belonged. With the added weight on his shoulders and a few extra pounds in his wallet, it would be interesting to see how the quiet lad from the back streets of Tbilisi would react. City needed to come flying out of the blocks this time around to settle the fans' nerves but despite the encouraging pre-season form, the curtain raiser to the 1997/98 campaign began disappointingly with a 2-2 draw against Portsmouth at Maine Road. Three days later and a Coca Cola first leg, first round defeat at Blackpool set the alarm bells ringing. Gio was in top gear for the 3-1 defeat at Sunderland, winning man-of-the match plaudits for one particular sustained spell of brilliance but a 1-1 draw with Tranmere, a penalty shoot-out loss to Blackpool and 2-1 reverse at Charlton left the Blues struggling in the bottom six. It was Groundhog Day again.

Yet again, the papers were full of rumours about Kinky's future and Franny Lee must have been tearing his hair out at yet more unsettling stories about his protégé were published on an almost daily basis, particularly after his hard fought negotiating during the summer. But there seemed more credibility to the stories linking Liverpool and Everton with moves for the player and the rumours would trundle on and on for the next six months or so. Howard Kendall was believed to be desperate to sign Gio and was prepared to break the bank to do so; but many believed Liverpool held the edge on the Toffees because of the Georgian's boyhood love of the Anfield club. The Merseyside rivals had been trailing the player with personal checks by managers of both clubs – there was even a suggestion that had Steve McManaman left for Barcelona at the time, Liverpool would have used the bulk of the £12m to prise Kinkladze away from Maine Road. But Macca's move never materialised, though he later signed for Real Madrid. It seemed no matter what Georgi said or did, in the eyes of the tabloid sports reporters, he was going to leave sooner rather than later and if transfer rumours didn't unsettle him, they would find other ways.

A fine win at Nottingham Forest should have been backed up with a win at Bury but Gio picked a bad time to miss his first penalty for City with his shot smacking the foot of a post. He almost made up for it by beating almost the entire Bury team in an effort to make up for the miss but the end result was a 1-1 draw. A first home defeat in living memory to Norwich City began to turn the tide against Frank Clark and his unimaginative style. Gio flew home for international duty shortly after, the crowd's jeers of derision from the last home game still ringing in his ears, even though the barracking wasn't aimed in his direction. He helped his country to a 1-0 win in Moldova before jetting back to Manchester for the visit of Swindon Town in the league. One thing had been proven since Kinkladze's first game for the club in that when he was good, he was exceptional and City invariably won. Sometimes he was just in the mood to turn it on and the Swindon match was a perfect example. With just two minutes on the clock, Gio stepped up to take a free kick that was fully 30 yards from goal. He ran up and struck a beautiful curling drive past Fraser Digby for the first of the afternoon. It was a perfectly executed free kick and just what City needed to give them a jump-start. From then on he tormented the visitors with, on this occasion, plenty of help from his team-mates and seemed to beat at least five players in one slalom-type run that saw his shot cannon off the stanchion and out of play. City won 6-0 – surely their season was finally about to take off...?

Chapter 12

CARS, GIRLS AND SUN 'EXCLUSIVES'

"I said to Gio before the season began that we should wait until Christmas and if things weren't going well for the team and he still being man-marked and getting battered, we'd re-look at things."

– Francis Lee

A red Ferrari 355GT, costing more than £100,000 was the first piece of extravagance Georgi allowed himself following on from his lucrative new contract in the summer. For the young man from a country still recovering from civil war and widespread poverty, it was a dream come true to own the type of car he'd imagined himself behind as a youngster. Cars like that back home were few and far between and owned either by wealthy businessman of members of organised crime. Gio was neither and had earned his personal dream machine by his talent on the football pitch but officials at City were secretly horrified when he turned up in a car that seemed to invite problems.

On the back of his magical display against Swindon, nobody would have argued if he'd have turned up with the crown jewels on his head but a fast car for a single young man in a city that averaged a 30mph speed limit still didn't sit easily with club officials. Back on the pitch, the annihilation of Swindon was quickly forgotten as, typically, the Blues followed up that potential platform by failing to score in the next four games and slipping even further down the table.

Then, a day before the glamour trip to Crewe, and having barely owned his new car for a month, Gio lost control at the Four Seasons roundabout in Hale and crashed into a motorway bridge. The car was a write off and Gio was thrown clear onto a busy road by the impact, somehow escaping serious injury but receiving 30 stitches in his back for a nasty gash. He could have quite conceivably have been killed in the crash and there were soon suggestions that it wasn't just a case of losing control of the car with rumours of Gio racing teammate Nicky Summerbee out of a hotel car park. Meanwhile, Gio was inundated by get-well cards and letters from concerned fans, worried about his well-being. The accident had obviously left him badly shaken and hardly surprisingly affected his next few appearances. He was well-below par when he returned to first team action against Port Vale just over a week later. Then *The People's* Phil Shirley again broke a story that once again had Gio talking freely. This was a journalist with either a great source, or a good basic knowledge of the Georgian language but either way, his stories seemed to always hint at Kinky being unhappy with something or another.

In his latest report, which appeared on November 9, 1997 – two days after a shocking 1-0 home defeat by Huddersfield Town – was in response to Frank Clark's admission that he would sell Kinkladze if he felt the need and was certainly not scared to do so. "There is a line to be drawn," the paper quoted Gio as saying. "I love this club but I would be deeply hurt if they sold me for the purpose of buying new players. That is not the way I want to go. I want leave of my own free will. One day they say how much they want me to stay, the next they are saying they might get rid of me." Gio went on to explain that his relationship with the fans that had "treated him like a king" was the main reason he was so reluctant to leave. For the first time, too, his best friend, Shota Averladze publicly voiced concerns about Georgi's situation at City. Averladze's wife was quoted as saying 'they knew he was not happy at City and he was concerned the club's plight could eventually damage his career'. Gio denied the comments as being misquoted but the story did seem perfectly plausible. Whether Gio was wrestling his own demons or not is hard to say, but the fact was, his next half-dozen games were a mixture of brilliance and anonymity with many starting to wonder if the constant man-marking and punishment he was often on the receiving end of was making his life a misery. It's easy to say he was being paid to put up with whatever treatment came his way but in the end, he is only human and just playing football seemed to have become secondary to making it through 90 minutes without a serious injury. He had already taken more knocks aged 24 than most footballers suffer during a whole career yet missed precious few games for City – a testament to just how tough he was.

The question was how many more horror tackles, shirt pulling, elbows, verbal abuse and sly punches could he take against the likes of Port Vale, Sheffield United and Huddersfield – all teams well equipped for the physical demands of the league if nothing else. Losing 3-1 to Stockport County at Edgeley Park, with City having their own fans on their backs was about as low as it got and barely a year into his job, it seemed as though Frank Clark had already lost the plot and any side prepared to mix it with the Blues usually ended up walking off with all three points. Kinkladze still rarely received protection from his teammates and there seemed to very little retribution handed out by his colleagues on the perpetrators.

As each game passed, Blues' followers began to wonder when, not if, Gio would finally leave for the bigger stage his skills deserved. It was, at times, frankly, embarrassing to see him surrounded by players who weren't up to the job. Ged Brannan, Jason van Blerk, Barry Conlon, Tony Scully and Tony Vaughan… the list of journeymen footballers went on. It seemed so typical of the club that they should perhaps have their best ever talent in their worst ever team. Four defeats in five league games had pushed Clark to the brink but the last thing the chairman wanted to do was have to replace yet another manager after such a short period of time.

As if things weren't bad enough, towards the end of November proof, if it were needed that Gio was now considered a big enough name to sell more copies of the nationals was when he was targeted for a series of kiss and tell sex scandal stories. Then he was linked with several other women as the media sought to paint him as the archetypal football 'love rat'. None of the stories are worth delving into because, as ever with these type of page fillers, there is very little substance to them and just one well-paid side of the story being told. Who cared if it was true or not? With the car crash, 'sex exposés', transfer rumours, the team's dire form and misquoted stories from Holland, his concentration levels were just about maxed out. For a man who took the most satisfaction just playing football, he must have wondered what he'd done to attract such negative coverage but it is maybe his reluctance to speak up for himself with the media, maybe through lack of confidence in his English, that compounded the problems.

Francis Lee admits that discussions had taken place between the player and the club about what might be the best for all concerned if City's hopes of promotion were looking hopeless by the turn of the year.

"For his final season, there were clubs interested in him from abroad because when you get coaches who are skill orientated, they want a player like Gio," said Lee. "I said to Gio before the season began that we should wait until Christmas and if things weren't going well for the team and he still being man-marked and getting battered, we'd re-look at things and do the best we could for him."

Things weren't going well and he was still being subjected to roughhouse treatment. The writing was not only on the wall but inevitably now also in the form of a written transfer request, which the Press was seemingly not made aware of at the time. By the start of the New Year, Everton had emerged as clear favourites to take Gio away from Maine Road in a deal worth about £7m. Howard Kendall was a long-time admirer and his already low popularity levels in Manchester dipped further with his bid to poach City's No.10 and on January 7, 1998,no less than four tabloids broke the news of Kendall's bid. Where the other stories had been little more than mischief making, this time, it seemed was a genuine bid had been filed and for the first time, Blues' fans wondered if their diminutive midfielder was finally set to leave. Chris Bart-Williams mentioned as a possible replacement... City fans held their breath.

The way things had been going at Maine Road all the stories, for once, seemed entirely plausible. Yet Everton were almost as cash poor as City and it appeared they needed to do a fair bit of wheeler-dealing to raise the necessary funds and besides, Francis Lee again poured scorn on the story saying it was 'all rubbish' and even if Everton did table an offer he would reject it. *The Sun* also led with a story on Gio, but for once, it didn't involve interest from another club. Instead, it claimed that Gio faced extradition following the police's decision to press charges for dangerous driving, which they believed caused the Georgian to crash his Ferrari back in October. The season was deteriorating rapidly on the pitch but off it, it seemed things were even worse. His best pal, Nicky Summerbee who had left shortly after the crash was also charged. Things could only get better and as the old year rang out, Georgi must have been relieved to see the back of his own *annus horibalis.*

By the time West Ham arrived for a fourth round FA Cup tie at Maine Road, Clark was living on borrowed time. It was a game when Kinkladze showed a national audience of millions watching the game live that two seasons playing in the First Division had done nothing to diminish his brilliance. Shorn of the second skin markers of some of the pub teams that City were facing week in, week out, Gio was magnificent and the whole team played with spirit and direction. Despite falling behind, it was Gio, who had already hit the bar with a rasping 20-yarder who brought City level. Receiving the ball out wide on the right he cut in, dribbled past three or four players before cutting back inside and planting a low shot in off the post and into the back of the net. Maine Road went wild and no doubt those watching from the comfort of their armchairs were once again enchanted by Kinky's skill. He continued to torment West Ham before Steve Lomas, now playing against Gio rather than alongside him, snatched a late winner for the visitors. As the Blues left to loud applause, few doubted that City's No.10 had played his last FA Cup game for the club but agreed that if it was, it was quite a swan song.

Three draws and a miserable home defeat to the mighty Bury later, and Frank Clark was sacked. The City fans feared the new manager's first job would be to sell Georgi Kinkladze to raise much-needed funds. And this time, they were right.

Chapter 13

BY ROYLE DECREE

"He would go down as one of the most fantastic talents I've seen and could do things most mortals couldn't even dream of."

– Joe Royle

Joe Royle, the man who had warned Tony Book and the rest of City's coaching staff that Kinkladze was a gifted player but would get them all the sack just a couple of years before, was installed as the new manager of Manchester City in what amounted to Francis Lee's last throw of the dice as chairman. Prophetically, the majority of City's coaching staff on duty the day Royle's Everton triumphed 2-0 at Maine Road, had now been relieved of their duties and Gio's future with the Blues was hanging by a thread. Royle quickly revealed that Kinkladze had asked for a transfer before Christmas to begin the attempt at severing the bond between player and supporters and criticised the Georgian's first display under his charge tutelage. "Georgi is a fantastic talent," said Royle after the 2-1 loss at Ipswich. "But he doesn't concentrate enough when the opposition has the ball. We need more from him in that situation."

Royle was cleverly engineering Kinky's exit through subtle, almost subliminal messages to the media. Indeed, David Bernstein, who was a member of the board when Royle first arrived recalls the new manager's first decision was to sell Gio.

"When Joe first came in, virtually the first thing he said to us was 'we will have to sell Kinkladze,'" revealed Bernstein. "He explained that it was for financial reasons but also because although he felt he was a great player, he felt he wasn't what we needed to get out us out of the problems we were in. I agreed with that and I approved it."

Royle had also made it clear that the Georgian didn't feature in any of his plans, as Francis Lee explains: "When Joe came in, we had lunch together and Joe's idea of playing football is completely different to mine. Joe and I are great mates but his idea of a football match and my idea of how the game should be played were worlds apart. He didn't like Gio – he said he didn't like foreign players who are tricky and do this, that, the other and I said 'Well, Joe, some of the best players in the world have been five foot nine and downwards and very tricky,' but he said that he wanted big, strong powerful guys in midfield who can get up and down, box-to-box.

"I said that was okay but it depended who you were playing. If you were playing against top class opposition, it's not good enough - you need to be able to play the game. But Joe is a wonderful manager for getting teams out of Division One and back into the Premier League – it suits his forte and he's bloody good at it. But again, we knew Ajax were lined up and I said to him well, it's great to have him in the team because if you want to get £5 million quid, just ring Ajax up and tell them, but Joe wouldn't play him in the team, anyway."

With Gio finally on his way out of Maine Road, Francis Lee also decided to call time on his tenure as chairman, handing over the reigns to Bernstein officially in March. Years earlier the former City legend had threatened that if he was ever forced to sell Kinky, he'd pack in the job and he'd been true to his word.

"It was an admission that your club is not really achieving what you want them to do because you have to sell your best player," said Lee. "I was criticised for selling Stevie Lomas for £3 million but if you look his record up, he's played 500 league games and not scored 10 goals – how can you have a midfield player who can't score goals? We had Garry Flitcroft who we sold to Blackburn – he was a great kid but we knew that if we were playing 4-4-2, if your four in midfield couldn't score goals, you'd need Jimmy Greaves and Alan Shearer up front to win you games."

Injury kept Gio out the next four games following an improved display in the 3-1 at Swindon but with Peter Beardsley signed on loan from Bolton, it meant Royle was in no rush to get Georgi back in the side. City won two and lost two of those games and were still in the relegation mire. In the *MEN*, Gio complained of a "dirty tricks" campaign being waged against time. One Sunday paper had said he was angling for a move to Liverpool. Fed up, he said: "I just wish the rumours about me would stop so that I can concentrate on my main concern which is playing for Manchester City and helping them avoid relegation."

In his absence, fans wondered if he was injured or being lined up to join somebody else. It appeared Royle wasn't too concerned either way. He'd clearly made his mind up the crowd idol was going one way or another and to be fair to the manager, he was doing what he felt was right for the club, though perhaps Georgi deserved at least the chance to prove Royle wrong. Then came the fixture that effectively spelled the end for Georgi Kinkladze as a Manchester City player. City were away to Port Vale, a physically intimidating side that could match or out-muscle any side in the division and with City's reputation for having a soft centre, it looked a mis-matched fight from the off. Of course, the

Blues should have been beating teams like Vale out for sight but this was a game when Royle's men had to stand up and be counted. Gio was passed fit and pitched into the team with Royle sending Beardsley back to Bolton. "He said we were too similar," said Beardsley. "Gio was fit and my time at City was over. I would have like to have stayed longer and thought I was going to but it didn't work out that way."

Vale Park was a mudbath and the 5,000 travelling City fans were in no mood for anyone without total commitment to the cause. The atmosphere was ugly from the start, with the visiting fans booing several of their own players – Uwe Rosler, Ged Brannan, Neil Heaney and Kit Symons had all become targets in the past few months – before a ball was kicked! When Martin Foyle put the home side on 13 minutes, it really was a case of unlucky for some. Arguments flared amongst the Blues' followers and there were several scuffles. Even Kinkladze, previously all-but untouchable, didn't escape criticism, with some claiming his heart wasn't in it anymore while others had come around to Royle's way of thinking that perhaps the time was right for the player to move on. In fairness to Gio, he didn't look fit and was tired of having lumps kicked out of him – he was desperately unhappy. For his legion of fans, watching him that day was a painful experience. True, world class players should be able to perform anywhere at any time, but stick Thierry Henry, Denis Bergkamp or even Zinedine Zidane in the City team that day and there would have been no difference. The time was right for Georgi to leave – everyone knew it. City lost 2-1 to Vale and nobody escaped the wrath of anger from the supporters. Royle chose to axe Gio from the next six games – he had laid the all encompassing spectre of Kinkladze at Vale Park and knew he could do pretty much whatever he liked from there on in. The Blues won just twice in those six games and continued to spiral towards the trap door. With Georgi in the team it seemed there was a struggling team with a potential match winner. Take him out of the side and you had a struggling side with little imagination and creativity.

During that time, Ajax came in with a bid of around £3.5m, which was turned down flat by the Blues. But the Dutch were determined they were going to get their man and Ajax boss Morten Olsen was phoning the player constantly to convince him that a move to Holland would be the ideal place to re-launch his career and the Dane was prepared to build the side around his precious talent . Negotiations would continue over the following weeks but Georgi, who Royle claimed was out of the side because he "wasn't in the right frame of mind" was still frozen out. Ian Bishop, another former crowd favourite had been re-signed just before the transfer deadline to bolster the midfield but the Blues were still on the brink of Second Division football for the first time in their long, proud history. Supporters couldn't understand why Gio was being ignored at such a crucial time. Results had proven that by taking him out of the team, nothing improved whatsoever.

Ajax returned with another offer for the midfield star and City's new chairman recalled how he and the board held firm and played a spot of 'call my bluff' in the process, ultimately benefiting the club to the tune of £2m.

"I handled the dealings with Ajax from start to finish," said David Bernstein. "When I became chairman, the club were in a very poor position. That in itself created a huge problem but also a great opportunity. I was given *carte blanche* by my board and the supporters to do whatever

I had to do to get the club back to where it needed to get and we took a lot of hard decisions. Because of the support I was getting, I wasn't concerned about the impact of selling Kinkladze because he had after all been part of a very unsuccessful team and the fans recognised this.

"They loved him as a player – as did I – but realised it was probably the right time for him to go. I personally handled all the negotiations and they went fairly smoothly until Ajax offered less than we were asking for so we walked away and even if I say so myself, it took a lot of courage to do that because we were so desperate for the money. It was a make or break deal for us and it was an awful lot of money involved but they came back, agreed to meet our price and the deal was done and I was very proud of the way we held our lines. There were no other clubs that came in for him during that time."

Gio travelled to Amsterdam to discuss personal terms and the Dutch giants agreed a £5.5m fee with City but Royle, sensing the fans' unrest suggested he might possibly include Gio for the last two games of the season. If City won them both, they would be safe.

Kinkladze was given a heroes' welcome when he was announced in the starting line-up against QPR, the Blues' last home game of the season. In the tunnel, prior to the team running out, player coach for QPR, Vinnie Jones, is believed to have begun winding Georgi up. Eventually, the Georgian decided he'd had enough and he lunged for Jones, with the players having to be separated by teammates. Within a few seconds Jones, once booked after four seconds for trying to take Peter Reid out of the game, was left looking the fool. A foul resulted in a City free kick and Gio placed the ball down 30 yards out, ran up, struck the ball sweetly and sent a curling shot past the QPR keeper for the opening goal. Gio turned and gave the V-sign to Jones as he ran back to the centre circle. The crowd went wild and, for a moment, it seemed like the old days again. Of course, it wasn't, though and the Blues soon fell behind to comical defending and a couple of awful decisions by Martyn Margetson and a spectacular own goal by City's Jamie Pollock. Gio went off after an hour looking shattered to sustained applause. It was the last time he ever played for City at Maine Road. The match ended in a 2-2 draw meaning that for the last game, the Blues' destiny was out of their hands, just as it had been at the end of the 1995/96 season. They needed other results to go their way as well as beating fellow relegation candidates Stoke City at the Britannia Stadium. Even with Kinky's mercurial skills, he alone couldn't get them out of this mess.

Then there was a further blow to the Blues' survival hopes. Georgia had called him into their squad for a meaningless friendly in Tunisia the day before the trip to Stoke, effectively ruling him out of the final match of the season. But Georgi was determined to play some part of the match at Stoke and after some hastily planned arrangements, instigated by former chairman Francis Lee who, despite something of a sour end to his tenure at Maine Road, clearly still wanted to everything he could to help City avoid the drop.

"I wrote David Bernstein a letter saying I couldn't understand that they were going down and their best player wasn't even considered for selection," recalled Lee. "He was playing in Tunisia for Georgia the weekend City played Stoke and I said that they should send over a private plane over for him and get him back in time for Stoke. Gio had told me he didn't want the club to go down and he wanted to play and do whatever he could to help out and I told them if necessary, I'd pay the travel expenses. They took a bit of notice and did exactly that."

City announced that Bernard Halford would fly to Tunisia to bring Gio back in a specially chartered jet. He hadn't, it seemed, played his last game for the club after all but it was going to be quite an operation to get him back in time as Halford recalled:

"I went out to collect him in Tunisia because the game against Stoke was so important to us. He was playing for Georgia against Tunisia 24 hours before the Stoke game. We'd hired a laser jet and flew to Marrakech Airport and went straight to the game to watch him play. After the match, I walked across the pitch after speaking with officials and stewards and went straight into the Georgian dressing room, which upset them a little, because I overstepped the mark a little. I'd gone in to let Gio know I was there but when I knocked on the door the coach was talking to the team and he wasn't very happy about my interruption, which I can understand.

"But I had to make sure I didn't lose Gio because I didn't know what the Georgians had arranged afterwards. Layachi, who worked with me at City and could speak Arabic, was long with me but there were still obvious communication problems. I had a job to do which was to get Gio back to England as quickly as possible and I needed to clear all obstacles to make sure I did just that. I also had to make sure there was no back door the players could leave from! As it happened, he came out shortly after and we had a car waiting. We rushed him back to the airport and flew him back to England.

"The amazing thing about that day was that we arrived at the ground where the game was taking place but had missed the kick off. We'd ordered tickets, picked them up and made our way to our seats. The area we were designated in had these seats that were like comfy chairs - and not fixed to the ground, either - so they carried two big armchairs in for me and Layachi to sit on and as we sat down, Gio did one of his magic runs from inside his own half, beat three or four men and from 35 yards chipped the Tunisian goalkeeper for the only goal of the game. It was as if he'd waited for us to arrive!

"We flew back to Manchester – there was only the three of us in the cabin. We had some sandwiches and tea and chatted about this and that but he knew it was probably his last game for City and he was quite sad about that. He had such an affinity with the fans and he wanted to make sure he played his part in the Stoke match. He'd played not to get injured in the friendly and he knew this was pretty much the end of the road. When we touched down, I drove him to his house to pick some clothes up and then set off for Stoke where he joined the rest of the team at the hotel. It was around midnight and he went straight to bed while I chatted briefly with Joe Royle. That was it and as far as my part, it was mission accomplished. I was sad that this was his last game and like everyone else, I loved Gio and though I have to wear two hats, one official and one as a fan, I loved everything the lad did."

City strode out against Stoke doomed to relegation. The other teams, Port Vale and Portsmouth needed to win their games to send City down, but the Blues had to do their best and hope that things went their way. Royle's men indeed did their best and won 5-2, beating their opponents with the kind of ease everyone knew they were capable of but Portsmouth and Port Vale had (all-too predictably) won comfortably as well and the Blues were relegated. Gio came on as substitute for future talismanic hero Shaun Goater, on 73 minutes to a fantastic reception but they were to be his last few minutes in a Manchester City shirt. As the team left the field, Gio, tears in his eyes, applauded the fans that he said had made him feel like a king and threw his boots into the crowd before finally disappearing into the dressing rooms, exhausted by the events of the past few weeks. Within days he was officially an Ajax player.

Joe Royle himself left Maine Road in May 2002 and later took on the role of manager at Ipswich Town but despite the press reports to the contrary, he says he never had an agenda with Georgi and he says he never really fell out with him. Whereas many felt he had a preconceived plan to get rid of Kinky, Royle denies this was true.

"It wasn't as black and white as that," he said. "Like everyone else in the game I knew he was a fantastic talent and I arrived hoping that we could fit him into a system which might save us from the drop. I know that Alan Ball and Frank Clark before me had tried the same thing but the big puzzle with Gio was that he didn't really have a true position unless you allowed him to be totally free when the opposition had the ball.

"In training, all I could see was this amazing talent but the facts were irrefutable that City had gone down two seasons before and were on the verge of going down again and he hadn't been able, for some reason, to do anything to stop it. There was a theory that some of the players who were at the club at the time weren't good enough to play with him but I looked at a similar position with Matt Le Tissier at Southampton where his goals kept them up for many years."

Royle and Kinkladze were together at City for only a few months and the former Blues' manager says, contrary to newspaper reports at the time, he liked Gio as a person and maybe under different circumstances, things might have been different.

"It was a shame because he was a nice personable lad who was no trouble but we actually worked together for a very short period of time – it wasn't even 20 games," Royle reflected. As for the nightmare at Port Vale that split many City fans down the middle as to whether Kinky (or the entire team for that matter) were up for the survival scrap they were clearly in, many, including the writer of this book, felt Royle put Kinky into a no-win situation that day, which considering the wage Gio was on, Royle was entitled to do. But if ever there was a case of horses for courses, Vale Park was it.

One could imagine the likes of Le Tissier being rested by Ball, Berkovic being left out by Portsmouth and David Moyes putting a inexperienced Wayne Rooney on the bench for such unpalatable looking match. So was Royle actually saying 'here's your hero – see what worth he is in a game like this?' or was it just a case of playing the best team he had available? Of all the question marks around Gio's Maine Road career, this was surely the pivotal moment that determined his future.

"I would have loved him to have been the right man for that team and there's nothing more I would have loved than for Manchester City to stay up," said Royle. "I wish I could have been the one to have got the best out of him but for whatever reason, it didn't happen and when he was sold in the summer, it helped us finance successive promotions."

Yet the stories of the pair's poor relationship continued for several weeks after Gio's departure. *The Mirror* carried a story claiming he flew out of Manchester upset and unhappy, claiming he could have saved City had Royle used him more often.

"I think if Royle had given me more chances to play we wouldn't have gone down," Gio is quoted as saying. "I think I could have kept City safe – I really believe that. I am positive it wouldn't have happened. And if City had stayed up I would have still been with the club – most definitely.

"I would have been happy to stay with City but once we were relegated, it became impossible for me to remain. The Second Division would have been very hard for me to play in and I couldn't have played there.

"It's a very sad day for me. I had good times at City but I had bad ones, too. I am very upset that I am going. There were moments when I was really unhappy. I won't forget the last day at Stoke when we went down. I admit I cried. That day hurt and I was so upset, too, during the time Joe Royle left me out of the side. He never gave me a reason why he wouldn't play me. Maybe I feel a little bitter – upset with the manager.

"But he's the boss and he knows his business. I am just so sorry to say goodbye to the fans because I love them very much. They are in my heart and that's breaking right now. I am going to a big club in Holland but I will need time to forget what has happened to me. I love City and the people and it's very hard for me to go, but I have a new life. I have signed for Ajax for two years but after that, who knows? Maybe I will come back."

The general tenor of all the 'Kinky Blasts Royle' stories, and they were plentiful, was that he was stating his opinion that he felt he should have been used more in the run-in. There was very little blasting done in Royle's direction. Yet whether the then-City boss was fooled into thinking there was is unclear. The papers were desperate to stoke up a good ruck, as they had been all along. Kinky and Royle hating each other made good copy and sold newspapers. At the time, though, Royle is quoted as firing a couple of volleys back in the direction of Gio.

The Sun perhaps carried the most venomous attack. In one article, Royle is quoted as saying: "His (Gio's) parting shot was like all his others – delivered from a long way out and hopelessly wide of the target. I'm afraid Gio seems to find the truth elusive at the best of times. Shortly after I arrived at the club he decided he had an ankle injury, but the truth is, he didn't seem to want to train.

"The first day I was there I took him aside and told him: 'Great players are great trainers and great players win things.' I know – I've played with some great players. He claims he could have kept us up but he had three seasons at City to make his mark and during that time the club was relegated twice and struggled the other season. To say he would have put it right this time is wide of the mark.

"He started three games for me and in two of them he was anonymous. In the other he was abysmal. That was at Port Vale and any City fans who saw him will know about his commitment."

It seemed the papers had their story.

The People then based an 'exclusive' on a 'senior City source' – nameless, of course, who revealed several earth shattering 'facts'. In bullet points they revealed that coaches and players were asked to applaud certain things Gio did in training; that he had Sunday lunches with Francis Lee; had a Mercedes from the sponsors and had other Georgians signed to keep him company. Gasp! Stop the press! What scandal! Perhaps, having heard the almost legendary skills Gio displayed in training people wanted to applaud him… is that not even a possibility? Is a roast beef dinner with the man who has become your surrogate dad that odd? Top players get top cars and whilst Mikhail Kavlashvili never really got going at City, Murtaz Shelia and Kakhaber Tskhadadze were more than useful players – let's face it, when it came to poor players arriving at City during Gio's time, these were three of the better signings. In short, there was no story, just column inches to fill. If Royle did get sucked in by the media at the time, today, he has no hard feelings towards Gio and perhaps realises he was hoodwinked into saying some of things he did at the time.

"Georgi and I are fine and we have spoken since," revealed Royle. "In fact I got a message at Ipswich that if we were looking for someone, he'd have loved a trial with us. That was at the start of last season but we were particularly strong in midfield at that point. The problem will always be with Gio is what happens when the opposition has got the ball? In the modern game, you have to ask whether you can afford to have someone who has no defensive input at all. I know Frank Clark played him off one striker and others thought his best position was behind two strikers and some of played him in an totally midfield role but it's still a puzzle as to what his best position is and I'm not sure Gio knows himself, actually."

The recurring 'best position' argument has surfaced many times in various debates about Georgiou Kinkladze but it seems clear to most, particularly those fans who watched him at Maine Road for three years, that his best position was simply allowing him to play wherever he wanted to. A precocious and rare talent such as his shouldn't be pigeonholed but allowed to roam freely. Perhaps the man who did more to keep Gio at

City during what was largely a torrid time for the club and player should have the last word on his time with the Blues.

"He was such a wonderful player for a striker who was a good mover off the ball," said former chairman Francis Lee." In fact, from our point of view, he was heaven sent. Every team needs a playmaker and I just think he was unfortunate that the team was struggling for three or four years and he came into that struggling side. Then suddenly, when he began to make things happen, Premiership teams started sticking a man on him and began to clatter and kick him and basically doing anything to stop him playing."

Does this say more about how we play football in England, especially when faced with a high degree of individual skill? Whatever the answer is and however many people attribute City's demise or non-success with Gio in the team, it is important to take into account his team-mates, many of whom, at times, sat back and waited for Gio to create something special or win games single handedly, whilst doing little to protect him as he was battered and bruised all over the pitch. It should also be noted that he played under a succession of managers in a very short space of time, many of whom had no idea how best to use his talent. It's been said before and will be said again, no doubt, that Kinkladze was the right man in the wrong team. City have had few better talents in their ranks and during the period he played for the club, they had few worse teams. This is a fact often forgotten when discussions about Kinkladze take place.

Chapter 14
RED WHITE AREA

"All I do know is that if you pay more than £5m for a player he ought to get a chance."

– Georgi Kinkladze

Still mentally drained from leaving the club he would have happily stayed at for the bulk of his career, Kinkladze, now aged 25, arrived in Amsterdam hoping to restore his reputation as one of Europe's most exciting players at one Europe's finest football clubs. True, it had been many years since Ajax last lifted the European Cup, but their reputation, built on the 'Total Football' theory – each and every outfield member of the team being able to play comfortably in virtually every other's position – was second to none. The likes of Johan Cruyff and Marco van Basten once graced the Angels and now Gio, a graceful and enchanting talent, had the chance to display his skills in European competition at long last. Domestically, however, the Dutch Erie Division was hardly on a par to the Premiership with only three or four teams ever seriously competing for the title each season. In many aspects, both Ajax and Kinky had a lot of catching up to do when it came to underachieving in recent years.

The summer had begun with some good news for Gio with his dangerous driving fine reduced from £2,500 to £1,000 at the Manchester Crown Court on appeal. The size of the fine was probably not the issue but there was a general feeling of injustice surrounding the case with the fact that this was a top footballer crashing a Ferrari perhaps clouding the vision of the prosecutors in the original case. Gio also won the costs back, too.

There was some good news for Manchester City fans, too. New chairman David Bernstein revealed that the Blues had first refusal when Kinkladze next became available. It helped ease the pain for the City faithful that reckoned Maine Road was going to be a duller place without the Georgian maestro pulling the strings in midfield, even though they accepted things had to change in order for Royle to resurrect the fallen Manchester giants.

"Our supporters have a special affection for Gio and he is a man with a great talent," said Bernstein. "We thought it was sensible to negotiate the right to first refusal. We are looking a long way down the road when hopefully we will be in a better position and circumstances will have changed."

Meanwhile, as a last hurrah, the media speculated the worth of Kinkladze's new contract at Ajax. While the *MEN* suggested it was a sober £15,000 per week over two years, other papers speculated wildly over the figures. *The Daily Star* reckoned Gio was about pull in £45,000 per week - £2.25m per year - with the Dutch giants. The actual pay packet, it was probably somewhere in-between. Gio's signing was announced on the pitch before Ajax's final game of the 1997/98 season and he was given a tremendous reception whilst a huge screen played some of his best moments at Manchester City. Everything seemed to be going smoothly though it would be fair to say that his progress had stalled in the last 18 months due to the predicament his former club had found themselves in during that time.

He played his first games in a Danish summer tour with Ajax beating FC Copenhagen 4-2 and Gio was amongst the scorers, as were such luminaries as Shota Arveladze, Ole Tobiasen, and Benni McCarthy. They lost the next match against the same opposition by the same score.

Gio was to wear the No.11 shirt for the upcoming campaign and team up with his best friend Shota Averladze, the Georgian striker who, ironically, had once been high on City's shopping list a few years back. Shota was a huge favourite amongst the Ajax fans and he remembered Gio's early days in Holland.

"I was already there when he came to Ajax –," said Averladze. "He never rented a house in Amsterdam, he just stayed with me. That's how close we are. When Ajax signed Kinky it was a total break with club policy – paying out such big money for a player. The Ajax way was always to bring up players from the youth set up, so spending the big money they did was very unusual. It showed how much Morten Olsen wanted him."

The Dutch champions had indeed long admired Kinkladze as Bernard Halford revealed:

"They paid just shy of £5.5m for Gio," he said. "They'd been tracking him for a couple of years so they'd done their homework. I've got to say that at the time, I didn't think moving to Ajax was a bad career move. They were one of the top teams in their country and also in the Champions League and that should have given Gio the platform he needed to really take off. Especially with the quality of players they already had at the club – as a playmaker, the team should have had everything they needed to complement his style of play. What more could you ask for?

"Plus his English had improved a great deal and the Dutch are great English speakers so there was no added language barrier for him. Gio had flown over to meet their officials and take a look around so he knew where he was going and he was happy enough with the deal. It's true we had the first option on him if he became available but it wasn't something we followed up or was ever really on the cards at any point."

Georgi had promised that if he played against Manchester United in the Champions League and scored at Old Trafford, he would lift up his Ajax shirt and reveal a City shirt underneath – if only! But the months ahead would be every bit as unhappy for Gio as his last days at City had been and this time he didn't have a legion of fans to lift his spirits – far from it, in fact. The move, in short, was about to turn into a nightmare and through no real fault of his own. The problems began when well-established Ajax hero Jari Litmanen's move to Barcelona fell through. Litmanen was the playmaker for the Amsterdam club and it was he Gio had, in effect, been signed to replace. The Finn agreed to stay another year and the focus switched away from the new record signing from City to a man the crowd already worshipped. It didn't take a genius to work out that two players couldn't fill the floating role behind the strikers and it appeared there was no way Litmanen would be sacrificed. So Kinkladze faced up to the prospect of playing out of position – or at least the position he'd been told he'd been signed to play in – for at least one of his two-year contract, perhaps longer. It was a huge blow, but not one he couldn't recover from.

But when Ajax boss Morten Olsen, whose constant telephoning to Gio had convinced him to sign in the first place, was sacked early into the new season, things looked bleaker still. The new coach, Jan Wouters, planned to play him on the left wing or, as it transpired, more often than not, on the bench.

"He has always felt that going to Ajax was a mistake," said Gio's brother-in-law Koba Bekeria. "You know, he was the most costliest transfer in their history? During the summer he moved from City and before the deal was finalised, Morten Olsen was calling him every morning on the phone, trying to persuade him to sign, telling him how amazing he though he was.

"The plan at the time was that Litmanen was going to move to another club – Barcelona or Liverpool, I think, and they wanted to bring in Gio to replace him. In the end, Litmanen ended up staying for another season. But by that time Gio had already signed.

"He played a few games for them, and then Olsen left. When the new manager came in he told Georgi he wanted him to play on the left side of midfield, not in his central position. And most of the time he was on the bench."

Franny Lee was still talking with Gio regularly and he was in no doubt where the blame lay for the player's lack of success on the pitch.

"He was unlucky that it was Ajax that he went to," opined Lee. "The coach that bought him left after six months and the new coach that came in played him on the left wing and the one side you don't play him on is the left, because if he's on the right, he can cut inside on his left foot and turn people inside out."

When Richard Burgess from the *MEN* travelled over to Amsterdam to do a catch-up piece on Gio, it became clear that what should have been a dream move for former City star was rapidly turning sour. He still hadn't found a home six months after signing and apart from his old friend Shota Averladze, he had few other friends in the city. Worse still, his few appearances for Ajax had done nothing to convince the Dutch fans that their record signing was worth the fee or the wages he was commanding. In his interview with Burgess, reading between the lines it was obvious he was deeply unhappy.

"I would like to get a house but I haven't seen anything I like," said Kinkladze. "It's no fun living in a hotel but at least Shota is around to keep me company. It is different here from Manchester – we can walk down the street and hardly anyone recognises us." When the reporter asked him directly whether he was happy he replied: "I would say I was 50-50. I miss Manchester and all my friends over there. I am planning to go back and watch City this season when I get the spare time. It took me a long time to get over relegation last season and I would still like the chance to say a proper goodbye and thank you to all the City fans. If things don't work out for me in Amsterdam I would like to return to England but I cannot look that far ahead at the moment – my aim is to be a success at Ajax. Mind you, I will admit my dream is to play with City again in the Premiership."

Averladze confirmed Gio's misery: "After six months at the club Olsen left and Wouters came in. Wouters wanted him to play wide left. He was never happy there. But Litmanen, the number 10 – who was a great player for Ajax – was already in the centre so it was always going to be tough for Kinky to displace him.

"Personally, I believe he could play any position, but he was determined he only wanted to play in the centre. I remember once at Ajax, Olsen was taking a training session; Olsen wanted to get him putting in crosses from the right. That was no problem for him, but he kept putting in really awful balls. Olsen was really annoyed. Later Kinky told me that he did it on purpose, so that they would make him play in another position!

"He never got a chance to play in his best position at Ajax. But then, even Michael Laudrup – who was their greatest ever playmaker - ended up playing on the left. Gio felt sick at Ajax. He hated everything there. He even hated Amsterdam, which is crazy really, as it's an incredible city, and now he absolutely loves it and flies over there whenever he has free time. But then it was different. As a player, when you're not getting to play everything else can seem wrong.

"But he was stuck at Ajax. Having paid out all that money for him, they needed to get some of it back. You can understand their position – it was a business transaction – but it was very tough for him. All he wanted was to come back to England."

It wasn't all doom and gloom for Gio and the brightest moments since his move to Holland had been provided by, typically, Manchester City fans that had made the journey over to watch him train or play for Ajax.

"Quite a few City fans have been over to see me and that has been nice," he said to Burgess. "Even after training there are people walking around wearing City shirts and wanting to speak to me."

One such bunch was a large party from one of City's liveliest supporters' clubs, Prestwich and Whitefield, led by the irrepressible Don Price. Amongst the pilgrims who set off by coach to for a weekend in Amsterdam was Noel Bayley, editor of the now defunct City fanzine *Bert Trautmann's Helmet*.

"City weren't playing this particular weekend and a coach-load of us travelled over with the intention of some of us going to watch Kinkladze play for Ajax," said Bayley. "But we didn't arrive until later than scheduled due to delays and diversions and by the time we got to the Ajax stadium, the game was already halfway through.

"So there was no way any of us were going to get to see Georgi play. The next morning we began in the bars quite early - as you can imagine with the P&W Blues – and there were two camps, basically. There were those who wanted to visit the stadium and the rest who wanted to hang around in Amsterdam.

"Five or six of us set off on a pub crawl and later on in the evening, we headed for the bar where we'd all arranged to meet up again. As we approached, one of the lads who'd travelled over with us was by the entrance and he said 'Georgi Kinkladze is in there playing pool.'

"We went in to this long, dark bar and at the very end was a couple of pool tables and sure enough, there was Kinky sat on one, signing autographs for what looked like the whole bar. Somebody had lent him the 1998/99 black and yellow striped away shirt, which of course he never wore in action for City, and he was sat there, proudly wearing it. He looked really happy and was clearly pleased to see all the City fans again.

"Apparently he'd seen the P&W Blues 'delegation' at the stadium and they'd let him know where they'd be later on if he could spare the time. He'd said he would try and get down if he could and he was as good as his word."

If Gio's mind was clearly elsewhere, it seemed to be evident on the pitch, too, with Burgess noting Gio was a shadow of his former self, anonymous in the game he watched and then embarrassingly, the Ajax fans cheered when he was substituted. Of the fans canvassed after that game, one said he reckoned Gio had played well for the first five minutes of his debut and then had done nothing since, adding that he didn't think Kinky had the all-round game to make it in Holland. Another Ajax young fan named Litmanen, Dani and Averladze as her favourite players but when asked about Kinkladze she half-heartedly replied, "Oh, he's all right."

By the start of the New Year, Wouters had placed Kinky on the transfer list. He was omitted from a South African training camp for the Dutch champions after events had clearly taken a downward spiral and forced to train with the club's youngsters. The relationship was at an all-time low between player and coach and the damage irreparable. The English Press were full of speculation of who might make bids to bring a player most Premiership sides would have loved to have had in their team just twelve months earlier. Despite City's first refusal on the player, there was clearly no way Joe Royle would ever have him back in his team where things were now beginning to tick along nicely and the status quo had changed at several of the clubs who were potential suitors a year before. Kevin Keegan, a long time admirer of Kinkladze had quit Newcastle and Ruud Gullit was now in charge at St James' Park. And Liverpool, constantly linked with Gio whilst he was at City, had, ironically, lined up Litmanen for the summer of 1999 and as Gio had learned, there was only room for one of their type of player at any one club. Merseyside neighbours Everton were another Premiership side that had continually tracked Kinkladze in his days at Maine Road but had now changed manager. Howard Kendall had gone and Walter Smith's hands were tied financially due to a proposed take-over battle at Goodison Park.

In April, *The Sun* carried the story that Spice Girl Mel C was prepared to pay £3m to make Gio a Liverpool player and stop him joining Everton. "This is not a gimmick," said a 'friend' of the singer. "She is deadly serious about it. Melanie loves her football – and Liverpool in particular. She is appalled at the prospect of Georgi joining Everton when her own team are searching for a ready-made replacement for Steve McManaman."

Of course, nothing ever came off and Gio remained at Ajax for another eight months, training with the youngsters and playing for the reserves before Jim Smith and Derby County came to his rescue. There was fall-out on both sides from the way things had worked out in Holland with suggestions that Gio simply couldn't adapt to the 'Ajax way', but surely the question mark should be with the Dutch for not doing their homework in the first place. Here they had a player who could create things from nothing and yet they were more worried about whether he could slot in at full-back if it was required – it has to be said that position is everything with Kinkladze and he went to Amsterdam to play in his natural role behind the strikers – that was how Olsen had sold the club to him in the first place.

"He had to do all the things he hadn't been asked to do in Manchester," revealed former assistant Ajax coach Bobby Haarms. "He had to defend, for example and was just part of the team.

"We were so excited when he signed but I never saw any of the good things I saw of him at Manchester City. At Maine Road, he was a god and could do no wrong but here things were different. I ask myself now if he was fit for Ajax and I'm not sure. Either he did not understand what we wanted or he just could not give it. Either way, his mental approach did not seem to be right."

Litmanen remaining at the club undoubtedly holds the key to why Gio's move to Ajax was doomed to failure. A mere dozen first team games is not much return for £5.5m worth of talent, yet it seemed Litmanen to Ajax was exactly what Gio was to the City fans. The No.10 shirt he'd been promised was returned to the Finn, who still was keen to pursue a career in England, let's not forget. Gio was in turmoil, desperately homesick for Manchester, pretty much alone living in hotel rooms or with friends and being asked to do things on the football pitch that must have left him asking 'Why?' What you see is what you get with Georgi Kinkladze – you never saw Red Rum walking kids across Blackpool sands and Gio pinpoints what he believes was the main reason behind the Ajax move turning sour.

"If I had known Litmanen was staying at the club I would not have gone there in the first place," he said. "That was one thing but overall I don't know what went wrong in Holland. All I do know is that if you pay more than £5m for a player he ought to get a chance.

"I never got a chance under Olsen and certainly not under Wouters. It was a terrible time for me and I would never play in Holland again. It's not that I have anything against the country but I will always look at it and think about what happened."

By the time Litmanen finally left for Barcelona at the end of Gio's first season, it was too late. Too many opinions had been formed and too many bridges had been burned. In fact, in a city where everything Ajax is obsessively covered, the news of Georgi's loan move to Derby was tucked away amongst the small print.

At the time, Gio's move to Pride Park came like manna from heaven. "It has to get better," he said. "Recently, my parents have stopped talking to me about football and only ask about other things. It got too painful. But I the summer I went home to Georgia and you know what I did? I played football with my friends – and I had more fun than ever."

His old mate Nick Summerbee was as surprised as anyone at the Dutch disaster. "I thought when he went to Ajax that that was his stage," he said. "He was a proven international and I thought he would really go on and show what he could do on a world stage but it didn't work out for him. If other clubs had been interested in him before he left, he kept it to himself."

Now Georgi had a chance to rebuild his career – he was still only 26 and could still live at his old home near Manchester. Derby County may not have been Manchester City but to him, they were the next best thing. He packed his bags and quit Amsterdam for good. It may have only been a loan move, but he was never going to go back and play in Holland again.

Chapter 15

SAME OLD KINKY

"Given the right players and right support, he will keep you up."

Francis Lee

Derby County were a club not dissimilar to Manchester City in that their glory years were the best part of three decades ago. They were obviously a smaller club in terms of gates and overall tradition but they were certainly one of the Premierships more engaging outfits, with a smart new stadium in Pride Park and a very much family orientated club with a loyal fan base that rarely dropped below the 20,000 mark.

Jim Smith, one of the most popular managers in the history of the Premiership had been the Rams' boss since 1995 but there was a real threat of relegation hanging over the club as the halfway point for the season approached. Just three wins out of 18 games saw the Rams third from bottom and Smith knew he needed somebody who could capture the fans' imagination and ignite his team back into somewhere near their true potential. Smith felt his midfield lacked invention and within two days had signed two playmakers on loan deals. The first, Avi Nimni arrived as an unknown quantity from Maccabi Tel Aviv on November 25 and a day later it was revealed that Georgi Kinkladze was also arriving – on a three-month loan deal – news that was greeted with much enthusiasm by the Derby supporters who knew all about the Georgian's reputation.

Gerald Mortimer was the Derby County reporter for the Derby Telegraph from 1970 through to 2002 and he remembers how the story first broke and the general reaction at the time.

"It was a curious arrival," mused Mortimer; "for a start; I'd always check any transfer rumours with Jim Smith and there would always be one of two reactions he'd give: 'No! That's absolute crap!' was one and the other was 'Aye, aye, he is one we've talked about'. I sometimes asked where the deal was with the player in question was up to and occasionally he replied 'Well actually he's sitting across the table from me!'

"The first I knew that Kinkladze was definitely coming was when I was up at Raynesway and he was there training and I thought 'what's going on?' Ajax were obviously were desperate to get rid of him but I believe Derby chairman Lionel Pickering virtually told Jim Smith and the chief executive that if they didn't get Kinky they were sacked! They ended up paying £3million, which is about £2million more than they needed to, in my opinion – I know Ajax had paid over £5milion for him but he was training with the youth team, I believe.

"I recall his debut as a substitute at Highbury and I thought he did alright. The ball was never going to bounce off him, was it? But from my point-of-view, I just thought he was the wrong player at the wrong time. Derby were really the in the trenches at the time, and declining rapidly, and you don't look for a muck of nettles from him, do you?"

Though Mortimer may have had his reservations, Smith felt he could get the former City star back to somewhere near his best with the right training and man-management. He had, after all, seen what he was capable of first hand, just a couple of years earlier.

"I first saw Georgi playing for Manchester City against Oxford United," said Smith, affectionately nicknamed The Bald Eagle. "I was doing radio commentary that day and I think at that time both clubs were in Division One. That day, Georgi gave a wonderful exhibition of his talents and completely ran the game from the first minute to the last, scoring two goals and maybe making another couple.

"I was managing at the time but still doing some media work on occasion. Later, not long after I'd taken over at Derby, I discovered he was available and of course, I was very interested. He's an exciting talent and a top player. Things hadn't gone well for him at Ajax and Franny Lee, who is still very close to Derby County, and a big believer in Georgi's ability, mentioned to my chairman Lionel Pickering that he was looking to return to England and he passed that on to me. My chairman asked: 'What do you think about Georgi Kinkladze?' I said, 'Let's go and get him,' but the price was three million quid so I suggested we got him over to have a look at him, on loan initially and we could take it on from there."

Smith also called his old mate Franny Lee, perhaps needing somebody who he knew would tell him what he wanted to hear to rubber stamp the deal. Francis Lee recalls the conversation they had and exactly what he told the Rams' boss.

"Jim Smith called me and said, 'I've got a chance of signing Kinkladze, what should I do?'" said Lee. "He had one or two other players I felt could lock in on him and I said 'I'll tell you what he'll do. He will win you games you can't win and you'll draw games you thought you would lose and will always pull a rabbit out of the hat and given the right players and right support and he will keep you up.'"

Smith knew he had nothing to lose but meanwhile the Telegraph's resident Rams reporter Gerald Mortimer was adding two and two and coming up with four.

"Lionel Pickering was a huge fan of Kinkladze's and thought he was maybe the best player in the world and I suspect Francis Lee was boring one or two things into his ear," said Mortimer. "I'm very fond of Franny and it struck me that he might still be the chairman of Manchester City to this day if it wasn't for Kinkladze."

So a deal was arranged to rescue the player from his Amsterdam hell. He'd been ostracised by the Dutch side and his confidence and fitness weren't anywhere near their normal levels but Smith wasn't worried about that, especially after having his memory refreshed by Manchester City's erstwhile former chairman.

"We organised a three-month loan from Ajax to Derby but before I did that Franny showed me a video of Georgi putting top, top players on their arses. He actually did that first while I was at Derby in 1998 but by the time I saw it he'd signed for fucking Ajax! It was a brilliant video and he was such an exciting talent that as soon as I had the chance, I brought him back to England."

The Rams still had to arrange a work permit for the player and on November 23, 1999 the review panel convened in Sheffield to deign whether or not a player who had played precious little over the past 17 months and had lost his place in the Georgian national side. There were five panellists and one was Georgi's former manager at City Frank Clark. Fortunately, they'd parted on good terms! Interestingly, two of the written testimonials that were presented arguing for Georgi's case were from then England Under-21 boss Peter Taylor and the other was from none other than Sir Alex Ferguson! This is an extract from the government document that provides a fascinating insight into the make up of work permit applications:

The Panel were well acquainted with the player's ability from his previous spell as a work permit holder. He is, in their opinion, a player of superb skill and would be a tremendous asset to the domestic game. Kinkladze's move to Ajax of Amsterdam had been something of a disaster for him personally. He had been asked by Ajax to play out of position so his effectiveness was lessened. This led to him not being selected on a regular basis. This in turn meant he was then unable to command a regular place in the Georgian national team when previously he had been a regular and a star name within that team. He had also suffered a number of injuries, which limited his appearances for both Ajax and Georgia. This inactivity had raised doubts about his current fitness levels which could have a bearing on the impact he would be able to make in England should his appeal be successful.

Mr Smith explained that doubts over Kinkladze's overall fitness were ill founded although he was short of match fitness and he wanted to see how far his recovery had progressed before making the signing a permanent one. Derby County's medical team had examined him fully and declared him fit. Indeed Mr Smith declared that should permission be granted Kinkladze would be in the team squad for their Premiership game this Sunday. He stated that Kinkladze was a world class player whose ability to excite crowds would be a massive boost to the English game. In his previous time in England Kinkladze had become something of a "cult" figure with English crowds due to his extraordinary skills and ability to turn a game in an instant. His previous record in England was testament to the significant contribution he would make to the English game. He said that the Club had signed the player on loan to the end of the season but they had first option to sign him from Ajax for £3 million should the move be successful. Mr Smith was confident that he would be able to judge whether a permanent move was possible in a short time and therefore hoped to offer Kinkladze a permanent contract well before the end of the season. He also said that the Georgian coach had stated that Kinkladze would be an automatic choice for the national team once he has established himself with Derby County.

Derby also indicated that Kinkladze was due to marry an English national next month, which would remove the need for any further work permit applications should this be the case. The Panel were unanimous in their opinion that Kinkladze was clearly a player of the highest calibre, would make a significant contribution to the English game and that a work permit should be issued to Derby County Football Club.

Steve Nicholson is the current Rams reporter at the Derby Telegraph, but back in 1999 he was still the sports editor and with the paper the one constant source of information for the Rams fans, he knew the worth to the club – and the paper – of Kinkladze's arrival.

"At that time the signing of Kinkladze was particularly exciting for Derby County," Nicholson recalled. "He was a big-name player who captured the imagination of the supporters because of the style of football we'd seen from him at Manchester City. We had all seen the television clips and the goals he'd scored during his time at Maine Road.

"The thing with Derby is they have a rich history and, of course, they won the old First Division championship twice in the 1970s – something that is unheard of and never likely to happen again with what is, essentially, a small English club. Derby is very much a football city and when people like Kinkladze, Ravenelli and Stimac arrive at the club, everybody sits up and takes notice. Basically, Georgi's arrival sent a real buzz around the city.

"When he first arrived on loan, everyone wanted to see him and see what he could do and many wondered how fit he was after playing so little in Holland. Derby were in the Premiership and I think it was about three or four months before they spent £3m to make the deal permanent. People weren't clamouring for replica shirts with his name on because, unlike when Ravenelli arrived a little while later, he wasn't their player yet and was only on loan at that point. Nobody knew if they'd buy him outright."

It's true that Georgi looked to be carrying a few extra pounds when he began training with his new team-mates – hardly surprising considering his exile at Ajax - but despite this Smith was determined his new capture would play some part in the next Premiership match for Derby. It's hard to imagine a tougher venue than Highbury where the Rams faced Arsenal to make your debut, but despite Kinkladze's lack of match fitness, he was named as a substitute while fellow new boy Avi Nimni was named in the starting eleven.

"What was he like when he arrived at Derby? His normal bloody condition – unfit!" laughed Smith. "But I remember his first game for us at Arsenal where I put him on the bench because, to be fair to him, he hadn't been playing for a while but he came on and held the ball up well for us and did well."

Arsenal had several top stars missing for the game but included Thierry Henry who was yet still to prove himself as an adequate replacement for Nicolas Anelka – how times would change! But despite the loss of David Seaman, Patrick Vieira, Lee Dixon and Martin Keown and Freddy Ljunberg with injury, the Gunners still represented formidable opposition.

With an hour of the match gone, Derby had led through Dean Sturridge's early strike but now trailed 2-1 thanks to the (still unproven!) Henry and Smith decided to haul off Nimni and see what his other new arrival could do. An air of expectancy went around both sets of supporters at Highbury with perhaps Arsene Wenger, rumoured to have had talks with Kinkladze prior to his move to Holland, as interested as anyone else in how Kinkladze would perform.

Kinky wasted no time when he received the ball, stepping over two challenges before spraying the ball out to Sturridge who fluffed the opportunity. The home fans began to get nervous every time Georgi received the ball but despite some lovely dribbling and a couple of dangerous through balls, Derby still lost by a single goal. At least they carried some new optimism forward after pressing the Gunners enough to have maybe earned a point.

With another week's training under his belt, Smith decided to give Kinkladze his full debut the following Saturday, leaving Nimni on the bench. A near full house of 29,455 fans packed into Pride Park to see Derby take on Leeds United and all the pre-match talk seemed to be about Kinkladze. The in-stadium TV, Vision Rams, showed a montage of his best moments at City and at one point, virtually a whole concourse, packed with fans enjoying a pint, fell silent as they were reminded of what their new midfielder's was capable of. It was fair to say he had the majority of Derby fans eating out of the palm of his hand before he'd even kicked a ball at Pride Park.

Kinky had a quiet first half but bedazzled the home fans with some more trademark dribbling and came close to scoring twice in the second half. It was a measure of his countrywide popularity when he was substituted on 75 minutes to rapturous applause from both the Derby and Leeds supporters. The Rams lost 1-0 and were still deep in trouble but there was a good feeling around Pride Park as the home fans filtered out into the early December evening. They believed their team could pull away from the bottom and for the majority that was purely down to the arrival of Kinkladze. He is perhaps one of only a few footballers who could make such an instant impression on supporters. He is the archetypal fans player.

A miserable 1-0 home defeat in the League Cup a few days later was anything but inspirational and Georgi was relegated to the bench for the next game at Leicester. New striker Branko Strupar made his debut as a second half substitute against the Foxes but Gio was unused as the Rams recorded a fine 1-0 win.

Whether he'd been running on pure adrenaline for his first two games or not is unclear but Smith opted to give the Georgian little more than 30 minutes play over the next five games as he set about getting him back to peak fitness. By February, Derby were making a fist of their survival battle and Kinkladze, who Smith had explained the absence of through lack of match fitness, was looking sharp again in training.

With half an hour to go against a resurgent Sheffield Wednesday side, the Rams trailed 1-0 and Kinkladze, thanks to the demands of the impatient home support, was drafted off the bench to try and inspire a recovery. Within minutes Wednesday led 2-0 but the game was far from over. Kinky took the game by the scruff of the neck and began to tear Wednesday apart, setting up Strupar on 85 minutes only for Wednesday to breakaway moments later and restore their two-goal lead. With two minutes left it looked a wasted effort but somehow the Rams scored twice more to record a morale boosting 3-3 draw and Georgi had won his place back in the starting line up. A 2-1 win at Everton followed and a draw at Sunderland kept Derby just outside the bottom three. The good form continued and already Jim Smith was talking about making Kinkladze's stay permanent and following the next game – a 4-0 victory over Wimbledon – the Derby fans were demanding the club buy him, whatever the cost.

Kinky was outstanding in the win, pulling the strings throughout and capping a wonderful performance with his first goal for the club. Three successive losses followed and time was running out for the Rams, but two wins and three draws out of the next six hoisted them up to sixteenth and that would be their final league position of a rollercoaster season.

Francis Lee was invited to the last home game of the campaign – a 0-0 draw with Newcastle United and there was a relaxed, happy atmosphere around Pride Park with Derby safe from the drop.

"I saw Jim at the end of the season and Gio had helped Derby stay up," said Lee, who'd predicted as much the previous autumn. "I went to see how Gio was getting on and saw Jim Smith afterwards and he said, 'Come and have a drink with me after, pal – thanks a lot!'"

Derby signed Georgi up for £3 million following his loan spell and that equalled the previous transfer records set by Seth Johnson, Craig Burley and Branko Strupar. He penned a three-year contract and at last could settle down again in England concentrate on his football after the best part of three seasons' worth of uncertainty and misery. But life at Pride Park was bizarrely set to mirror his days at Manchester City in an uncanny and unnerving way over the coming years.

Chapter 16
THE BELIEVERS

Whatever it was about Georgi Kinkladze, he had instantly cast his magic spell over the Derby faithful just as he had done at Manchester City. A hernia operation in July disrupted his pre-season training and kept him out of the first three games of the 2000/01 season, none of which the Rams won, but he was considered fit enough to be on the bench for the first game of September – a home clash against Middlesbrough.

The atmosphere was electrically charged and many put it down to the fact that Kinkladze, who had taken over Rory Delap's No. 10 shirt, was back in the squad with his move from Ajax now permanent. He seemed to have mesmerised the home support into believing anything was possible once he stepped on to the pitch and with 65 minutes of the game gone and the Rams 3-0 down, he was brought on along with another crowd favourite Malcolm Christie, also returning from injury. The effect the pair had was incredible and thanks to Kinky's vision and Christie's finishing, the game ended 3-3 on a memorable evening at Pride Park.

But the rest of the month didn't quite pan out so well with two defeats and two draws in the next four league matches. Kinky played in two and was substitute in the other two but against Leeds he restored the faith by coming off the bench on 73 minutes and scoring a wonderful goal.

He weaved his way past Ian Harte and Oliver Dacourt before slipping the ball deftly past Nigel Martyn just two minutes later to earn Derby a 1-1 draw. But with the Rams struggling again at the foot of the table, a section of the Pride Park crowd had begun to call for Jim Smith's head. Stormy waters were ahead.

October saw three games played and nine more points down the drain. The pressure on Smith was greater than ever an in an effort to stop the rot, he appointed former Derby stalwart Colin Todd as his right-hand man. Todd, was very much 'old school' when it came to defending and his mandate was to get the team playing tighter with more aggression and his thoughts on Georgi and his type of player would become better known further down the line.

The effects of Todd's savvy defensive tactics were immediate at the Rams enjoyed an excellent November, failing to concede a goal for the next four games before losing to Manchester United at home and then Fulham in the Worthington Cup. The win against Bradford City in particular saw Kinky at his very best, setting up both goals in a 2-0 win and proving almost magnetic for the Bradford players who often had three or four trying to get the ball off him (and inevitably failing). Gio later claimed the arrival of Nigerian star Taribo West had enabled him to play his more attacking game. Whatever the reason for his and Derby's fine form, their season was finally up and running and the pressure eased on Smith.

December was fruitful again, but Gio was missing from the first three games with injury and the Rams won two games 1-0 and lost the other at Chelsea 4-1 in his absence. He came on as a late substitute in the 2-0 win over Newcastle before being named in the starting eleven for the most emotional game of his Derby and perhaps entire career so far – Manchester City away.

A full house for the Boxing Day fixture at Maine Road was always a certainty, but there were thousands more who would have loved to have been there to see Gio Kinkladze return to his spiritual home, albeit in the colours of Derby County. He was given a fantastic reception from the City fans who had waited a long time to say 'thank you' and they chanted his name before the game and received the biggest cheer of all when the teams were announced before kick off. He received standing ovations whenever he took a corner from the fans in the North Stand and Platt Lane and was applauded by the entire crowd when he was substituted on 78 minutes. City were struggling, too and the 0-0 draw was far more valuable to the visitors than it was hosts. The Rams ended 2000 with a 1-0 loss at Southampton but they had at least pulled themselves up to sixteenth in the table and were one of the Premiership's in-form teams going into the New Year.

Loan signing Stefan Eranio was proving a popular player and his style was not dissimilar to Georgi's and this was obvious as the pair rarely started together, often one replacing the other. Gio played just one full game in January, missing the home return game with City, and missing three more through injury problems that were hampering his progress in the Derby side. After tearing a groin muscle in the 4-0 defeat at Middlesbrough he would miss the best part of three months before coming as sub against Coventry at the end of March. The Rams were still in trouble and the first three games he took part in after his return, all ended in defeat. Many felt he didn't look fully fit after his lay-off and his weight was a continuing topic of conversation amongst the Derby fans. His first full home game in four months saw him subjected to the type of pub tackling he hadn't endured since his second and third seasons at Manchester City and it all came courtesy of a certain Mr Robbie Savage, who, as the saying goes, had 'previous'. Kinky, no doubt black and blue by the time the game ended had the last laugh as his side cruised home 2-0, but losses at Bradford and Arsenal meant there were just two games left and still a chance of relegation.

A trip to Manchester United was the last thing Derby needed but a Malcolm Christie goal in the first half was enough to secure a victory and ensure the Rams' Premiership status for another season. They completed the season with a 1-1 draw with Ipswich, finishing in seventeenth, spot, and just one place out of the drop zone. Georgi's former club City weren't so lucky and returned to Division One after just one season back in the top flight.

It had been another draining season for all concerned at Pride Park and the feeling that Derby were just doing enough to survive didn't fill anyone with confidence for the forthcoming 2001/02 campaign. As for Georgi, he'd missed two thirds of the season with various knocks, strains and pulls and started just 13 Premiership games. It had been a tough and disappointing season for the Georgian who had shown brilliance occasionally, if not all the time. He'd won his place back in the Georgia national team after an absence of a year and he'd also married an English girl and become a father for the first time, his wife Louise having given birth to a baby boy, Sabba.

Jim Smith felt that because of the poor start his team had endured, Kinkladze's impact was somewhat diluted as Derby were forced to opt for a more blood and thunder approach to save their skin.

"I can't deny the fact that his biggest problem in the first full season he had with us was that running about and running your bollocks off was more important than the skill that Georgi had, unfortunately," said Smith. All in all, after the best part of five seasons in England and one in Holland, Georgi was still waiting for his first fully enjoyable, settled season outside of Georgia, but in Smith, he still had a major fan.

"He was a joy," said Smith. "The players loved him and admired his skill and Georgi had it in abundance. He was a very quiet lad – very quiet – but the lads loved him to death but he wasn't the most forthcoming talker in the game but he did a super job for us and we stayed up.

"In particular that season, I remember the game against Leeds when we went down to ten men and were 1-0 down when I brought Georgi on and then controlled the game and scored a great goal. He went out on his favourite right-hand side, came in on his left, did two players and bent it into the top corner. It was a great goal and a vital one for us. I loved him, like everyone else."

Gerald Mortimer from the Derby Telegraph, however, was still not convinced about Kinky's value at Pride Park.

"I thought he'd lost the ability to get away from people at Derby, something he definitely did at City," opined Mortimer. "For me, he'd lost that edge. He was a very personable guy – very quiet – almost shy and self-effacing. It certainly wasn't the wrecked sports car image we'd all thought of him before he arrived. He divided crowds, I thought. If he was on the bench, you'd always here 'Get Kinkladze on you twat!' – aimed at Jim Smith, of course.

"But he scored that wonderful goal against Leeds when he took the lot on and popped it in the net so some things he tried clearly came off, didn't they?"

In a game they say is all about opinions, many had few or none on a lot of players, but it seemed everyone had some kind of view about Georgi Kinkladze, good, bad or indifferent. When it came to the supporters, though, it rarely dropped beneath good and the new season would be a big one for Georgi. He had to return fit and sharp and consistently produce the goods in order to prove the doubters wrong once and for all.

Chapter 17
THE EAGLE FLIES

Since leaving Tbilisi and up to joining Derby, Georgi had enjoyed only one season where the manager kept his job and that was in his first year at Manchester City. Since then he'd watched them come and go apace at Maine Road and then at Ajax when he moved on. Since moving to Pride Park, only Jim Smith had been his boss and this was his third season with the club. Seeing the same man give the team talk for successive years must have been something of a novelty for him.

But the settled period was about to end.

One thing Smith couldn't afford was a bad start to the 2001/02 season after two consecutive and exhausting battles against the drop. The fans wouldn't allow it and the board's patience would be stretched to the limit. Gio was sub for the first game of the campaign but his appearance after the break led to a second decisive goal and the Rams beat Blackburn 2-1. He was unused in the 3-1 loss to Ipswich but again climbed off the bench for the 0-0 draw at Fulham. Fabrizio Raveneli had signed in the summer and hopes were high that the 'White Feather' would profit from the likes of Eranio and Kinkladze's sublime passes. But neither Kinky nor Raveneli could unlock West Ham in another 0-0 draw though both players found the net in the Worthington Cup tie against Hull City, which ended 3-0. But successive league defeats to Leicester, Leeds and Arsenal left the Rams floundering again and Jim Smith decided he'd done all he could with a team that only played in fits and starts.

Two days before Derby were due to play Fulham in the Worthington Cup, he resigned and Colin Todd was promoted to manager on the same day. This wasn't good news for the club's flair players and Georgi Kinkladze in particular who was now faced with the kind of boss who preferred good solid tackler in the middle of the park and those who had a touch of genius better track back and get stuck in or else face the axe.

Predictably, perhaps, Gio was to play just 31 minutes of Todd's first four games in charge, none of which ended with a win, and a further slap in the face was the arrival of Benito Carbone, the skilful but vastly overpaid Italian attacking midfielder/striker loaned for three months from Bradford City who were allegedly paying him a staggering £40,000 per week.

There was no sign ok Kinky for the next four games either and fed up with Todd's attitude towards him, he asked for a meeting with the Derby manager with his personal lawyer Daniel Izza in attendance to discover why he wasn't being played. This most unusual story hit the headlines the next day and the Derby Telegraph's Steve Nicholson recalls the meeting vividly.

"It was very, very strange," began Nicholson. "It was late 2001, when it happened and we carried the headline 'Kinky Lays Down the Law' and the story was about Gio summoning his lawyer, Daniel Izza, in an attempt to win back his first team place. He'd had a meeting with Colin Todd who had been manager since October 10, 2001. He'd only played Gio once, as a second half substitute against Tottenham at White Hart Lane and he didn't play him for the next eight games.

"Todd wasn't a great success as manager and during the meeting with Todd, Izza told the Rams boss that Georgi was fitter than he'd ever been and was keen to play for Derby and believed he could contribute to the team and lift them out of the relegation zone.

THE STORY OF GEORGI KINKLADZE

"I don't think Todd was that impressed by it all and he said afterwards 'I've met Mr Izza and obviously Georgi was there. I also had a chat with Georgi and told him if and when an opportunity occurred he had to grab it and show us what he is capable of'. It was an old line, really and it didn't really make any difference."

Privately, Todd is believed to have been angered by what he considered to be a manipulative move by the player. He wasn't a Kinkladze fan to begin with and if the crowd favourite never pulled on a Derby shirt again he couldn't have cared less. During the infamous meeting Todd said to Izza "Georgi has to understand that is an art to tackling" – what chance did he have? Todd, just as Frank Clark and Joe Royle before him, liked a certain type of player and Gio just wasn't his cup of tea. Georgi arrived late for training one day and Todd asked him "How can you be late when you've got a Ferrari?"

Todd's sacking couldn't come quick enough for the Georgian, or the Derby fans, come to that matter and as an ironic twist, when Todd had used all his credits and the Rams were 1-0 down at Aston Villa, the travelling Rams fans demanded Kinkladze, actually named as one of the substitutes at long last, be brought. The doomed manager complied with just 21 minutes on the clock! Within two minutes it was 1-1 and guess who'd played a major part in the goal? Derby still lost the game 2-1 and Todd was dismissed shortly after and Carbone returned to Bradford a few days later. Caretaker boss Billy McEwan took over for two games in the interim and he used Georgi twice as a substitute in each match.

But there were better times ahead for Kinky when, on January 31, 2002, former Derby player John Gregory was installed as the new boss at Pride Park. He had Georgi on the bench for his first two games –

one win, one loss – but reinstated the one player who had the ability to not only lift the Derby fans to near hysteria just by taking his tracksuit top off, but also had the ability to win games almost single-handedly. Gregory was no mug and carried no baggage or preconceptions with him; he was a football man and he wanted the best players in his team.

Just three games into his Derby reign, Gregory seemed to have worked out how best to utilise the numerous talents at his disposal and the Rams turned in a stylish display at Leicester, winning 3-0 with a goal from Kinkladze, who was subbed seven minutes from time and earned a pat on the back from his new boss. Impressive though the win was, it still left them second bottom with a lot of work to do, especially with Manchester United, Arsenal, Bolton, Everton and Chelsea to face in the next five games.

Gregory was getting the very best out of Kinky who had added a tremendous work-rate to his undoubted repertoire everybody the Rams could pull clear of the relegation places. The Telegraph's Steve Nicholson was also convinced the Rams would survive.

"Georgi didn't play in Gregory's first two games as boss against Tottenham and Sunderland," he said. "He was in the squad but then started ten of the next eleven matches, scoring on his first appearance for Gregory in a win at Leicester.

"Derby were second bottom of the Premiership when Gregory took over and for a time, it seemed they would survive. They won two of the first three games under his reign and drew at home to Manchester United before losing 1-0 at Arsenal and then winning at Bolton, which was a massive result because they were struggling, too. Everyone thought that was it and they would go on to avoid relegation but Derby then managed just one point out of the remaining eight games and were relegated. It was a complete mystery and to this day, John Gregory has no idea why they dipped so badly.

Relegated to the Nationwide Division One for the first time in six years, the dip towards the end had been inexplicable but for Georgi, he faced up to his worst nightmare of First Division football again as the Rams unerringly mirrored Manchester City's fortunes with the Georgian in their team. A stubborn Todd had underused him and, for those who believe in superstition, he had made 13 Premiership starts for the second successive season. His first season had also ended with a total of 13 appearances – it really was a case of unlucky for Gio.

Life in the Nationwide just didn't appeal to the Georgian and echoes of the bruising encounters he'd suffered whilst at City must have haunted him all summer. But, the argument he was on good money was a fair point and he had signed a contract with Derby that would run another season. Yet the continuing and remarkable similarity to his time with City was about to happen again and pre-season favourites for promotion Derby were soon cut adrift in mid-table, unable to raise their game sufficiently to beat the more physical sides who just loved roughing it with the pampered millionaires.

Kinky missed most of the first half of the campaign either through injury or being dropped from the team. Gregory wanted no passengers and though the Rams' No.10 showed the odd flash of brilliance here and there, it wasn't until he returned to action against Gillingham on January 11, 2003. From there on in, he was largely magnificent and perhaps as influential as he'd been anywhere since his first season at Manchester City. Derby hit form at the same time Kinky did – coincidence? Three wins on the bounce before a trip to runaway leaders Portsmouth and a game few will Derby fans will forget. Steve Nicholson was there reporting for the Derby Telegraph and he recalls how, despite Derby taking a beating in the first half, Georgi turned in a spectacular second half display that almost produced a miracle.

"Of all the managers, I feel John Gregory got the best out of Georgi," said Nicholson. "It was during a spell which ran from January 2003 through to March when Gregory was suspended. The team were struggling and slipping badly but Kinkladze was outstanding and won four consecutive man-of-the-match awards. In a struggling team, he was very, very good. That period dispelled a popular myth that Kinkladze goes missing when things get tough – that was a tough period for Derby and he was their most prominent player and that taught me a lot about the player.

"During that period of time, Derby played Portsmouth away. Derby were 3-0 down after 22 minutes and Portsmouth were top of the table and flying towards the Premiership. Derby were on an alarming slide and Georgi could have gone and stood in the corner if he was a player who wasn't interested but he got hold of the game for about a 25 minute period either side of half-time and inspired Derby back to 3-2, scoring one himself, and Portsmouth didn't know what had hit them.

"For 25 minutes, he was world class and that's not something you can often say about players in the First Division. People might say 'well it was just 25 minutes' but those same critics would have been the ones who would have said he would go missing at 3-0 down. I would love to know what brought that out because he was sensational. Derby didn't quite get the equaliser and eventually lost 6-2 but it was an amazing performance and I will remember it for a very long time."

Despite Kinkladze and the squad's best efforts, there was just too much daylight between them and the play-off places but after the 2-2 draw with Sheffield Wednesday a week later, Gregory hailed the Georgian maestro for his superb form of late.

"He is an inspirational player for us," said Gregory. "He has made a massive contribution over the last five games. The rest of the team are probably his biggest fans; they appreciate he not only has great quality but he also rolls up his sleeves and works hard all over the pitch."

Yet six games later - five of them defeats – Gregory was suspended with Mark Lillis taking over for ten days before George Burley took over at Pride Park. Derby were fifth bottom and facing an unthinkable second consecutive relegation. For Kinkladze, this was too much like a recurring nightmare and he had made his mind up to leave Pride Park, despite a contract offer of a new one-year deal, and find a new home, preferably back in the Premiership.

"George Burley was Georgi's last manager at Derby and he was in charge for the last seven games of the 2002/03 season," said Steve Nicholson. "They needed to win at least three games from their last seven to survive and they managed to do that to stay in the First Division and Georgi played in six of those seven games.

"At the end of that season in May 2003, Derby had to cut their wage bill. So what happened was a lot of big names went or didn't have their contracts renewed. Ravenelli was one; Craig Burley was another as was Bracno Strupar and Rob Lee. Kinkladze's contract was also up but Burley wanted him to stay and offered him a new one-year deal. He'd just been crowned Player of the Year for 2002/03. It would have been a huge pay-cut, perhaps as a much as half the original deal and he probably felt he could get a better deal elsewhere so in mid-June 2003 he left the club.

"George Burley was disappointed in his decision saying, 'It was a very good offer from the club and it's a big disappointment to me and for everybody else that he has said no. He feels that his future is elsewhere and in the end you've got to respect that. We need people here who are one hundred per cent committed to Derby County.

"His agent Ivan Benis said: 'We are considering offers from other clubs in England and Scotland and we appreciated the offer from Derby but in the end we had to say no.'

"I feel he should have accepted the offer for another year at Derby. He was a huge favourite with most of the Derby fans – not all of them, but most of them – and at a time when things weren't going well for Derby, inevitably the biggest cheer of the afternoon would be when he was substitute and he leapt out of the dug-out and took his tracksuit off. The fans would chant his name when he wasn't playing.

"The last real memory I have of him was after his last game for the club at home to Ipswich. Georgi had been presented with his Player of the Year award before the kick-off and Derby went on to lose 4-1 and it could have been eight. After the game finished, the players came out for a sort of lap of honour but they nervously edged towards the centre circle – there weren't too many people left in the stadium, to be honest.

"The fans who had stayed were letting them know they weren't too happy but when Georgi appeared they suddenly stood and applauded him as an individual. Most of them loved him and for me it was strange because the admiration never matched the contribution he made. On the occasions it did, he stood out head and shoulders above everybody else and I've never seen someone who could deliver a weight of pass quite like him but he did frustrate you immensely because you wanted him to do it all the time.

"After he'd gone and Georgi hadn't fixed himself up and there was a suggestion that Derby should ask him back. Burley had a wafer thin squad and there was a feeling amongst supporters that they should re-offer the contract. I thought it was not the right way to go even though he was a flash of lightening amongst the storm clouds for many games.

"He is an extremely quiet individual – almost shy and some people mistake that for arrogance. On the many occasions I interviewed him I never found an arrogant streak, just a quiet, shy person who didn't appear to comfortable being in the limelight. He never sought publicity but he was quite an engaging character when you did get to speak with him and he was extremely well mannered. You had to really listen carefully because he was so quiet but most of the things he said made an awful lot of sense.

"He's only 31 and I find it sad that he isn't still playing for Derby. We have Ian Taylor, who was magnificent for Derby during 2003/04 and he's 36 and he'd be the first to admit he hasn't got half the indivudual skill Kinkladze has. He is a magician with the ball and perhaps only the great managers could utilise his abilities to their best. He was brilliant, but frustrating and never quite found his right role within the team.

"Yet for me, Georgi, when he played, always left you wanting a bit more. I think with talented players you always expect more and want a bit more. I watched him play and there was so many times he made things look so easy and then he may go quiet for a while. The managers knew he had ability, the fans knew he had ability and it was just getting the best out of him consistently that proved frustrating. He has always been searching for the perfect manager, in my opinion but maybe people expected too much of him."

Former Telegraph reporter Gerald Mortimer also remembered those last days at Pride Park and how the Derby public perceived the player.

"He took the Player of the Year award in his last year, which was odd considering he'd not played more than half of the games," said Mortimer. "Then he made the strange decision to turn down a contract and do nothing for an entire season at time in his career when he should have been playing. The local radio was very in favour of Georgi and I was never against him, I just couldn't see a function for him in the Derby side – though there ought to have been.

"I used to get very testy letters from a guy in Stockport who'd given up his season ticket at Manchester City and bought one at Derby and he always asked why I never gave Gio credit – I'd reply because I didn't think he'd done anything yet. He could control the ball, see a pass, weigh it – all the equipment was there, but his CV carries three relegations. I've always felt there wasn't a particular hole for that particular peg. For me, his potential is unfulfilled. You didn't half want what you knew he could offer. He was the sort of player who would always have been picked first in the schoolyard!

"Gio's time at Derby, for me, amounted to bits and bobs. My stance was always that there was a wonderful talent there but getting him to apply it on a consistent basis has defeated about eight managers in this country. My end comment is that I'm a bit sad that I feel we should have seen a hell of a lot more from him. At Derby we never really found the key."

Glasgow Rangers star Shota Averladze believes there was a simpler answer to Gio's lack of success at Derby.

"Derby were not on the same level as City in terms of size and tradition, and then, of course, they got relegated," he said. "After you've played against people like Bergkamp and Cantona in the top flight, it's hard to adapt to that level. And I believe that, like Bergkamp and Cantona, Kinky is a special player. The trouble is that not many teams these days have space for a player in his role, that 'free role'. If you look at the whole of the Premiership today for example, the only club I can think of is Bolton with Okocha. None of the bigger clubs... United, Chelsea, Arsenal – have anyone in the free playmaker role."

Francis Lee, who has continued to track Gio's career closely remembers a player whose career seemed to take a similar path as the Georgian's.

"When Gio was at Derby towards the end," said Lee, "they were selling the better players he was again left in a position where teams in the division could man-to-man mark him and kick him out of the bloody game. He's really had a very unlucky career so far. We used to have a player at Bolton called Freddie Hill who I got Malcolm to sign when I went to City to help boost the squad and he was 31 or 32 then. Freddie had a chance of getting away to Liverpool earlier in his career but for one reason or another, it never happened. If you ask anyone who saw him play they will tell you he was a brilliant player – he had Kinkladze's skill but he didn't get away at the right time and his career never got where it should have done. There is a time when everyone has to move on."

One of Georgi's biggest admirers during his days in white and black was his former manager Jim Smith who is obviously still very fond of the lad from Tbilisi.

"He was a cheeky little player but he knew his ability and worth and he'd just laugh at you if you said 'You're not fucking fit enough' or whatever," said Smith. "You had to work him a bit harder but he was a super guy, never problem and he wouldn't have a go when he was out of my team, he'd just get on with it. He did more good than harm for Derby, that's for sure.

"As for the clubs he's played for it's fairly simple; he loved it at City and hated it at Ajax. I didn't have that many in-depth conversations with him but you couldn't help liking him. In terms of his fitness and professionalism he was sometimes a bit lacking but I just accepted he was a genius. After all, we paid £3m for him didn't we? It was massive money to us – too fucking much!" concluded Smith, chuckling.

Gio returned to Manchester City for the final ever game at Maine Road against Southampton – ironically the team he had scored the wonder goal that made him a household name all over Europe. Part of the 'Parade of Legends', he was amongst 20 or so former crowd favourites who had been invited to the game by the club as part of the pre-match entertainment. When he was introduced to the Maine Road crowd, he received a tremendous reception.

"City is the one club dearest to my heart and wherever I go I'll always love and be grateful to the City fans for their support they gave me," he said before walking across the pitch to a deafening ovation. At City, nobody had forgotten Georgi Kinkladze and it was fitting the man who had scored the greatest ever goal at Maine Road should be there to see it off. How many wished he was heading down the tunnel to get changed for the game instead of going to take a seat in the stand.

Chapter 18
THE LOST SEASON

"Why waste everyone's time? He deserves a little bit more respect than that considering what he's done in the game."

– Nick Summerbee on Bolton Wanderers

Kinkladze left Derby officially in June when his contract expired, destination unknown. There was interest, as there always is with a player of his calibre, but there was no deal in place and for his numerous representatives, it was time to earn their corn. Surely a Premiership club or one of the big Glasgow clubs would make a move for a player who had just earned his third Player of the Year award in his six full English seasons and he didn't see as taking a risk at all. Lesser talents than his were arriving from abroad at a rate of knots and he knew he had to be patient.

Celtic did show a firm interest but were put off by what's believed to have been continued agent interference. Basically, Celtic were confused as to who was actually representing him and despite the fact they were looking for a player of his ilk, the proposed move never really got going as they rapidly lost interest at the various packages being quoted to them. Weeks went by, nothing solid was in place and if he hadn't joined a club in time for pre-season training, it would be tough to find anywhere at all. But he hadn't been forgotten by at least one man – Jim Smith. The Bald Eagle was now assistant manager at Portsmouth alongside Harry Redknapp and Smith reckoned Gio might be the answer to their vacant creative midfield position.

"I invited him down to Portsmouth to train with us after speaking with his agent," confirmed Smith. "We spoke on the training pitch but not much other than back stage. Harry Redknapp loved him – he was his kind of player also and we just wanted him to do well but he wasn't fit and we didn't have a lot of time. We told him 'You've just got to do it Georgi,' but I think he realised it wasn't going to happen and eventually he left us. He played one game in a pre-season friendly at Brentford and he did really well but he needed to get his fitness levels right up and we didn't have the time and I'm not sure he had the inclination, either. It was before we signed Eyal Berkovic and though Eyal trained a bit harder, Georgi is a better talent."

With the chance to play for Pompey gone, there was no way he'd be with a club for the first few months of the 2003/04 season. Then, in early autumn, Scottish Premier side Dundee contacted him over a possible move north of the border. They weren't the kind of team Gio had in mind but he was open minded and waited to see what they had to say. Former derby teammates Fabrizio Ravanelli and Craig Burley had already been tempted to Tayside by the empire-building plans of Giovanni Di Stefano, a fast-talking lawyer who was supposed to be revitalising the Scottish club with a big cash injection. Dundee manager Jim Duffy travelled down to meet Kinkladze in Manchester, and was genuinely hopefully that a deal could be reached.

Jim Connor, Dundee's ex-commercial director explained the club's interest in the player: "We were keen on him because of the Georgian connection that had been forged with the club. Temuri Ketsbaia, Georgi Nemsadze and Zura Khizanishvili had all been with the club previously and obviously we all knew Georgi was a wonderful talent. But when it came down to the nitty gritty, he had at least three or four agents surrounding him at any time and we couldn't work out what the score was. It was probably the worst case I've come across of different agents getting in the way.

"On the day the transfer window was closing, about an hour and half before the deadline, Georgi phoned me himself and said he thought the deal could still be done. But in the end the agents were the problem – he was getting bad advice. Manager Jim Duffy worked on it tirelessly to get a deal done as had everyone else at the club. But every time a new agent came on the scene the ante was being upped. Only after two weeks did we finally manage to speak to the guy who was his official agent."

But Georgi just couldn't shake the doubts from his mind and despite the chance to play football again in a decent league he decided still he had a chance for a bigger move elsewhere. Perhaps because of the way things ended at City/had been at Ajax/developed at Derby, he was nervous to make the plunge again in case it wasn't right for him - and it clearly didn't feel right. Back at Dundee, where Di Stefano was at the time claiming he had the power to lure the likes of Edgar Davids to Dens Park, it was an unwelcome rejection. "Kinkladze can forget it," he ranted. "And the rest can forget it – I don't play second fiddle to anyone so there's no chance of him coming to the club."

Despite having no club, this time Georgi got it right, as Shota Averladze explains…

"I don't think it was a case of getting bad advice," he said. "But it's maybe that he's been waiting for something bigger to come along. I've always said to him: don't dream; take what you have today, don't hold out for more. That was the case with Dundee. He could have gone there. But there was always the hope that Liverpool would call and follow up their interest. He trained there for a while, so there was a chance of that happening.

"I told him he shouldn't sit by the phone and should take the chance of a move. I told him he should go to Dundee and then if he was playing, and playing well, Celtic or Liverpool would come in for him. As it was he had a lucky escape with Dundee as they went bankrupt soon afterwards. But, if you see what I mean, Kinky didn't make the right decision, he became right as a result of what happened."

Imagined wage demands and rumours of weight problems was clearly making Gio's hopes of finding a club even harder. In an exclusive interview with the Daily Mirror, the clubless star opened his heart about his five-month absence from football.

"My contract at Derby ran out and the offer they made me for another two years was not for me," Kinkladze told reporter John Cross in October 2003. "Now I still have no club. It is very depressing and I never imagined it would be this hard. It's frustrating but I can do nothing about it.

"I want to play at a good level in the Premier League which is why I want to stay in this country and also because I love life here. I've turned down some very good offers from Galatasaray, Valencia and Steaua Bucharest because I want to stay in England. My time at Manchester City was the best of my career and I love the English game and the fans.

"But it is very frustrating training hard and keeping yourself fit when all I've got to look forward to is playing for my country when I would love to be in the Premiership. I've been very grateful for some people who have helped me. Jim Smith allowed me to go down to Portsmouth and train during the summer and since then it's been hard working on my own.

"I also had an offer from Dundee which I thought about but I still believe that I could do a good job in the Premiership and would be willing to have a trial or anything. I thought being a free agent during the transfer window is closed would help but nothing has happened yet. Maybe some managers do not like to take a chance on a player who is a bit different but I just need an opportunity."

Louise Kinkladze, Gio's wife also spoke to the paper, explaining how low her husband felt. "He just wants to play football," she said from their family home in Knutsford, Cheshire. "He's been so quite and down for weeks. With Georgi it is not about the money. He just wants to play. There have been a lot of hangers-on down the years who have tried to take advantage. They have all disappeared now."

There is nothing new about leaches sucking dry footballers because it's always happened and always will. It's up to the object of their attention to wise up to them or continue being little more than a cash cow for them. Privately, some of Georgi's close friends feel he's been the victim of several such types and none of them have done anything to help his career along.

"Too many people have been scared off Kinky because they think he's going to be too expensive," said Shota Averladze. "It could have been Kinkladze at Celtic. Martin O' Neill was seriously considering him as a replacement for Moravcik last season. But then O'Neill found out that he hadn't played for three months and lost interest. Celtic then bought Juninho, but they never play him.

"That's been Gio's problem recently, and I've told him as much: you're not a player if you're not playing. I think psychologically, after playing for big clubs like City and Ajax, the idea of going to a smaller club was tough. But that is the situation Kinky has had to face – it's tough, yes, but sometimes you take a step back to go two steps forward."

Around Christmas 2003, Georgi even made an impassioned plea to Kevin Keegan to let him come and play for Manchester City, but the Blues weren't interested. "I still love City and would play for them nothing," he said. Averladze reckons the old saying 'you can never go back' had something to do with the snub and thinks his path of going to a top club straight from Georgia ultimately didn't help his cause.

"Keegan never tried to bring him back," said Averladze. "He said – and I know this for sure - that he didn't want to bring in players who had been at the club before. You can't blame Keegan – every coach makes the decisions he thinks are best, Personally, I find it disappointing that City never made more effort to bring him back.

"Kinky had an easier journey into big league than rest of us Georgian players, who had to go to smaller leagues as a stepping stone into the top European leagues. I went to Turkey first; Ketsbaia went to Cyprus first. Now he is facing a tougher challenge, and he needs to come through it. I'm not saying that it was easy for him to adapt. He arrived when he was 21, didn't speak English, went straight into one of the top leagues in Europe, and was player of the season/played his best season.

"Staying at City when they went down was the mistake. I know there are a lot of City fans who still love him and who respect him for doing that, but it doesn't really help him now. He needs to get himself back to the top level."

Then, a few days into the New Year, Eddie Gray at Leeds offered Kinky a trial at Elland Road. It was an ill-fated exercise for the Georgian who had offered to play for nothing and if Leeds beat the drop, they could pay him a set amount of money, believed to be somewhere in the region of £250,000 – four months' wages and a lot less than many of the Leeds players were on. But he left after a few days with the Yorkshire club quoted as blaming his wage demands and his weight but many believe it all to have been little more than a publicity stunt by Leeds.

The trial, helped to be set-up by Georgi's lawyer Daniel Izza, was doomed from the word go, it seemed.

"They didn't have a penny," said Izza. "They were hoping they were going to get some money through a restructuring of finances but it never happened. The ironic thing was Leeds had a player who Georgi had helped shape the career of – Seth Johnson – who was sidelined through injury and was being paid an extortionate amount of money. But in the end, I don't think Georgi was even paid his expenses. He'd been totally professional throughout the trial and even stayed at a hotel at his won expense."

Quotes from the Elland Road club that they'd not taken Georgi on because he "was too fat" were unfair and cruel, though the 'Elland Road insider' remained unnamed.

"Georgi being too fat at Leeds is a load of nonsense," said Izza. "A week later I took him to Bolton and he weighed 71 kilos – 2 kilos over the weight he'd been when he first signed for Manchester City. He was pretty fit and I stayed on and watched him do the fitness test for Bolton and the guy taking the test said 'Not bad… not bad at all' when he finished. He told Georgi that players had come to Bolton who had not being playing at all and been in much worse condition. He played four reserve games for Wanderers but nothing transpired."

Bolton, with Sam Allardyce's reputation for rejuvenating players, had seemed the ideal club for Georgi to make his comeback with, but ultimately, the club decided that Jay-Jay Okocha was too similar in style and they also had Youri Djorkaeff at that point, too. For Georgi, with the 2003/04 season nearly over, it was just another kick in the teeth and by this time, he was finally thinking of playing football outside of the British Isles.

It seemed a dramatic return to Dinamo Tbilisi may be on the cards at one point, but he had stated many times in the past that he didn't feel returning home would be a good career move. It was painful not only for Gio and his family, but for his close friends such as Nicky Summerbee who was at a loss to explain why things had gone so badly since leaving Derby.

"When he was going to Leeds and all these other teams on trial, he just needed someone to sit down and tell him how important he was to the team," said Summerbee. "At City, the crowd did that for him each week and some of the managers did believe in him.

"He came back to Derby and apart from the odd flash of brilliance, he never quite achieved what he was capable of. We keep in touch, not as much as we used to, but I think he got a little bit upset towards the end of 2003 with the way things were panning out in England. You would think somewhere along the line somebody would have a go with him but nobody has or is willing to do that. People have this philosophy about him that he doesn't work hard – well make him work hard – that is what the manager is there for and Georgi will do whatever you want him to.

"It's down to the managers to get the best out of him. One of my mates who I play with, Andy Gray, asked about Georgi while his dad Eddie was manager of Leeds so I said 'why don't you get him down for a trial?' Leeds were delighted with him and everyone was in awe of him but then one day they turned around and told him he wasn't what they wanted. That was a bit strange. If the problem was his fitness, why not just get him fit? He was willing to play for nothing just to prove himself.

"Then he went to Bolton and I went down to watch him and he looked fit and sharp. He was on the ball and looked good and at one point he did this bit of skill that had everyone around me saying how brilliant it was and that's what Georgi is all about. That would have been enough for me and I would have worked with that alone if I'd been manager.

"Even if you just brought him on for the last half hour, everyone knows what he's capable of doing and he would be a great asset to have at your club but these people just wouldn't take a chance. At Bolton, he was there for a few months and then they turned around and told him he was too much like Jay-Jay Okocha – they must have known that to begin with so why waste everyone's time?

"He deserves a little bit more respect than that considering what he's done in the game. Georgi just couldn't understand why Bolton had treated him like that and he was very down about it. He could have signed for any number of First Division clubs but he wanted a team at the top end. What he needed was for someone to just take a chance on him but nobody has."

His close friend and former City chairman Francis Lee has kept close to Georgi since he left the Blues and he believes his love for City could possibly have resurrected his career in England had he been offered the chance of a trial.

"Gio would play for Manchester City before any other club in the world," said Lee. "He loves the club and he loves the people and I saw him 12 months ago when he was at Bolton on trial and he said 'Is there no way you can get me back there (to City)? I would play for nothing and prove myself and then I'd sign a contract.' I passed it on to the club but nothing came of it.

"I saw him when he was at Bolton. If Jay-Jay Okocha hadn't signed a new contract they would have signed Kinkladze and that again would have been a good break for him but you couldn't have Okocha and Kinkladze in the same side because you'd need two balls!

"The Premiership has changed so dramatically now with the amount of space there is in midfield, players like Gio would run riot. Gary McCallister had a great autumn to his career because as soon as they decided to kick the ball miles and the game opened up and left space in midfield, Gary went on to help Liverpool win three or four trophies when he was virtually finished. If you saw some of the great midfield players from then past you'd think they had come from Mars because they played in such a tight, restricted area."

Nobody doubts that with Gio still only 31 until this summer, he can still have a great end to his career I England, if someone will just believe in him.

"I'm sure he can go on playing at the top level for another four years," said Shota Averladze. "He's actually younger than me – by six months, and his kind of role can have a longer life span. He will never forget how to play football. What he's got is a gift that you can't buy or you can't teach. But it is down to him to make full use of the talent.

"His short-term goals are to get back into the national team early in 2005 and then a return to one of the major European leagues in the summer. Georgia have some big games coming up in the next year or so and hopefully Kinky will be part of those games and everyone in Europe will be hearing about him again."

Chapter 19

FRIENDS REUNITED

"My first real memory of Georgi is playing together for Georgia against Wales – I think that was our second game. We won 5-0 and he was absolutely fantastic."

– Temuri Ketsbaia

With no shortage of admirers overseas, Georgi Kinkladze finally packed a suitcase and took up the offer of one of his god friends to go and play football again. Former Newcastle United and Wolves star Temuri Ketsbaia, who had taken on the role of player/manager at Cypriot club Anorthosis Famagusta was only too delighted to have a talent like Kinkladze's on board and towards the end of 2004, Gio made his debut, scoring a goal and showing plenty of his trademark skill, if not a little rust. He scored again the following week and has settled in well, though he has had to leave his wife Louise and Sabba, now nearly four, behind in Cheshire. He is getting near to peak fitness and will use his time in Cyprus to launch himself back into contention for perhaps his last major contract in professional football.

"Going to Cyprus is just about getting his legs back," said Shota Averladze. "Having Temuri Ketsbaia as his coach is a good thing – he is also another of our old friends. And he will help Kinky in whatever way he can, but you also have to remember that he is just starting out as a coach, and has to think also about building his own career.

"If Kinky can get 10 good games under his belt in Cyprus he will be back in the frame. The level in Cyprus is decent, and there are some good players playing there. Anyway, the fact that he's in Cyprus won't bother Alan Giresse, the new Georgia coach. After all he's looking at players in the Georgian league, too.

"Everyone wants to see him back in the national team. Giresse coming in as head coach could be a really good thing for him as it means a new start. Giresse is not judging anyone on what happened yesterday, or on past reputations – that can be a bit tough on some of us older players, as everyone wants recognition for what they've achieved. But it is basically a good thing.

"I know what Kinky can be– I still believe in him. If he gets back into the national team it'll be a great thing for me too. In 12 years playing together, around 75 percent of the goals I've scored for Georgia have come from his assists.

"He thought about quitting the national team to focus on his family and club football. I remember talking him out of it. So then when I said I was thinking about giving up myself he got really angry with me. So now, I'm waiting for him to come back to the team."

Indeed, with Temuri Ketsbaia as his new boss, even if it is for a short period of time, Georgi could not be in better company. He has someone who already believes in his wonderful ability and knows first hand what he is capable of.

"Georgi and I are old, old friends – we go back a very long way," said Ketsbaia. "My first real memory of Georgi is playing together for Georgia against Wales – I think that was our second game. We won 5-0 and he was absolutely fantastic.

"We were together in England all those years, after all. He is a very special person for me. I knew he had had trouble looking for a club. So I called him up and asked him if he'd come in and help me. I'm very pleased he said yes, but that is the kind of guy he is. It's been a big boost for me and for the other players.

"He has already had a big impact. He scored in his debut and you can see that he is helping other players to play.

"You have to remember that he was very young when he moved to England. Twenty-one is very young. And Georgia is very different from England. Perhaps if he had been 25-26, already married with a family, it would have been easier in some ways.

"I've spoken with the Georgian football federation, and they are watching him very closely. If he continues to play the way he did last week, I'm sure he will be back in the national team very soon.

"When you have a player like Georgi, you have to play to his strengths, and base your game on attack. But football is not just about imagination and talent. You have to run for 90 minutes and you have to fight. Even the biggest stars in the world are expected to do that

"I still believe it is not too late for him. And I really hope he gets another chance to play in England. I've told him that if any offers come along, he is free to accept them. But for the moment I am delighted to have him here"

Gio's brother-in-law Koba Bekeria is also convinced moving to Cyprus was a good a move.

"I think he is a lot happier now, in Cyprus, because he is getting his form back," said Koba. "That was the main reason for moving there – not for the money, but to show he can get back to his former fitness levels. He will be there until the end of the season in May, I think.

"I know that his real ambition is to break back into the Georgian national team this March (2005). Alain has discussed it with him, and I know he is an admirer of Georgi's.

His sister Marina believes his future still lies in England: "He still regards England as his second home. After all, he's married to an

Englishwoman. He really wanted to stay and I think he would love to come back to stay in England. He feels at home there."

Georgi was forced to spend Christmas 2004 in Cyprus, despite his best efforts to return to Cheshire and enjoy a family Christmas with his family. His Georgian passport has caused him problems and delays for many years and Francis Lee believes there is only one solution to the problem.

"I've been advising Gio for years to get himself an English passport and get English nationality," said Lee. "I've told him he's paid more tax in this country than 99% of the people who live here so if anyone's entitled to a British nationality, it's him. I think he will become a naturalised Britain soon and have a dual passport.

"He's remained remarkably injury free and, despite what people have said, when I saw him last, he wasn't carrying any weight – he was barely 11 stone. Providing he keeps himself fit he can still be a very, very good player so long as he's playing in a team where players move off the ball and he can play his own game for the benefit of everybody else. He'll have that wonderful ability until the day he dies."

TRIBUTES & OPINIONS

"He would go down as one of the most fantastic talents I've seen and could do things most mortals couldn't even dream of but he was never really in a successful side."

Joe Royle

"If you are going to play him, you have to live with what he does. He's one of those players some people refer to as a 'luxury player' but he's much more than that and very effective with it. He'll never lose you a game and if you have a talent like that in your side you've got work around his ability. He's a tremendous player with the ball – he's not when he's not got it and everyone knows that – you give great players the ball more and have a bit of faith. You play him because of what he can do, not what he can't do. With Kinkladze, the focus always seems to have been on what he can't do – Matt Le Tissier had the same problem. If you don't provide the ammunition he can't do anything – I say give him a free role and let him do what he wants to do. He sees things others don't see and the crowd love him. Let the players play."

Neville Southall

"It did cross my mind to sign him but I saw him around that time and thought he was carrying a bit of weight and that's what put me off. People told me about three months later that he'd lost a lot of weight, knuckled down and he looked fit but I lost track of him to be honest, not because he wasn't in my mind but because he wasn't there. But ability wise there was no question of how good a player he was. He was a unique talent, different and I couldn't liken him to anyone I'd ever worked with and to work with him to you had to sacrifice certain ideals about the way game is played to fit him in -but therein lies the challenge."

Steve Coppell

"*When he left City, he felt it was the biggest mistake he'd ever made. If he could have stayed at City he would have. He would have loved nothing more than for City to have stayed up and him remain at Maine Road – it would have been ideal for him. It's just a pity the way things panned out for him.*

"*Things could have worked out so differently for him had we had a little bit more luck on the that last day against Liverpool. We would have stayed up and Georgi would have remained a Premiership player, which is the stage he deserves.*

"*When I was at Sunderland I met up with him and he had this video of things he'd done at City and I didn't realise just how many times he'd beaten three or four players in a dribble from the halfway line or some of the goals he'd scored.*

"*He was totally football and after training, he'd just go home and watch football on TV or something he'd taped. It was his life. It gets me mad when I think of how his career has gone so far and how it should have been. It's been okay but it should have been so much more. The sad thing is that despite playing really well for City, he's never fulfilled his potential. There are players playing in the Premiership today who aren't in the same league as Georgi but somewhere along the way, it just didn't go right for him.*"

Nick Summerbee

"*I think it was a great shame that he was somewhat spoiled at City and had he had a greater deal of discipline and less of being a favoured player, he would have been a lot better off – for me, that was the key. I think that he was such a talent, and so well regarded, that he was treated as a very special member of the squad and for any player, that is a slippery slope to be on and in that respect, it didn't him any favours in the long run.*"

David Bernstein

"As professional observers of the game, we become fairly cynical but Georgi was one of that rare breed who you would go and pay your own money to go and watch him play. He was the sort of player who could raise a cynical commentator from his seat. I just can't believe his wonderful goal against Southampton didn't win goal of the season. He's of an age where he should still be playing top-flight football. He didn't run with the ball, he glided with it."

Jon Champion

"He's the only player I've ever seen who could be running at full pelt and then stop dead. Most people carry on a few steps with the forward momentum but not Georgi. I was only with him at City a short time but it was long enough to know that he is a wonderful player."

Nicky Weaver

"He's my all-time hero because of the way he could lift the entire crowd to its feet and make the dark days brighter. A fantastic footballer."

Nedum Onuoha

"Maybe he had too much too soon. Coming from the poor country he did and enjoying the trappings of fame early on, who knows, but he's had a great career so far, also, we shouldn't forget that."

Jim Smith

"I was asked to do a photo shoot at Gio's house for an ill-fated Esquire feature. They were going to do a piece on City and David Conn, who writes for The Independent, was writing it. It was a kind of on-going thing they were doing and for me it was sort of an excuse to be involved with City in some form because back then, I had no real dialogue with the club. It had been arranged to do a stand-alone feature on Kinkladze and the only time he could do was over Christmas.

"I went to his house and his parents were over from Georgia and his sister was there too. His sister was great and while he was getting ready for his pictures, his sister was telling me all sorts of things about Gio's relationship with the club that she probably shouldn't have been doing!

"Gio understood a lot more than he let on, in my opinion, and he was just sat there watching some crap on Eurosport whilst his mum handed out walnut cake that she'd brought over from Tblisi with her. I went into the room where we'd arranged to take his pictures and it was totally dark apart from this 60 inch TV screen showing football from god knows where.

"I asked him to get ready for the pictures and he said he was going to wear black so I put black drapes over the curtains to get a dark shot. I had one light and my camera bag was in the middle of the floor. I turned the TV off and for a moment, it was pitch black. Gio walked in and tripped over my bag in the darkness and as he did he managed to twist in mid-air and land on the sofa. He looked at me and just said, "Penalty." I could have put him out for six weeks but he was very cool about it all. He was quite shy but just a really nice bloke."

Kevin Cummins

"I think Manchester City were definitely the right club for him, though perhaps there was also a point when he could and should have moved on in order to advance as a player, and win things.

"I've been around for a long time – I think I say this not as his friend but as a decent judge of football – he is without doubt the one of the best players in terms of natural talent I have ever seen. Perhaps he didn't always have the right advice – so many things are needed for a footballer to achieve their potential."

Temuri Ketsbaia

"He has never forgotten the fans at City. When Kevin Keegan first became manager at City he phoned Georgi up and asked him to come back. But Georgi was worried about coming back in case it didn't work out and he was blamed."

Marina Keberia (Gio's sister)

"Myself and my wife, Georgi's sister Marina, lived with Georgi for eight years in Britain – both in Manchester and Derby - and in Holland when he was at Ajax.

"Unfortunately, his later career hasn't gone the way he hoped, but he remains hugely proud of the fact that he played for Manchester City. He says that whatever has happened, that is one thing he will never regret. He still has the tapes of lots of his games and I've even seen tears in his eyes when he watches them.

"It's hard to say what happened. Sometimes fate works against you. It's not like he had any personal problems like Paul Gascoigne for example.

"It just seemed like he was cursed sometimes. And he would sometimes say, 'why is this happening to me?' On so many cases, when he was about to sign for a club, something happened at the last minute to spoil it – either they changed their mind, or signed another player instead. It has weighed on him mentally, though he is not one to talk about it. He tends to keep everything inside."

Koba Keberia (Gio's brother in law)

"I believe Kinky's biggest mistake, in terms of his career, was staying with City to when they went down. I know it was tough for him, the loyalty of the fans and the club meant a lot to him. And I know that a lot of people respected his decision, but I don't think it's doing him too much good now.

"I had a similar situation myself at Trapzonspor in Turkey. I had a great rapport with the fans, still adore them, and I still get a great reception when I

go back there. But I left to pursue my dream at a bigger club. Kinky lost a year by staying at City. Then they got relegated again. He could have done a lot more if he'd had that year at a bigger club.

"We're talking about a player who was good enough to play for Real Madrid. I think me and my twin brother, Revaz, have always been the most blunt with him. We tell him 'you're the biggest talent anyone has seen in the last 10 years, but that is not enough in itself.'"

Shota Averladze